The Housing Issue

ISSUES

Volume 181

Series Editor

Lisa Firth

Independence

Educational Publishers
Cambridge

First published by Independence
The Studio, High Green
Great Shelford
Cambridge CB22 5EG
England

© Independence 2009

British Library Cataloguing in Publication Data
The Housing Issue – (Issues; v. 181)
1. Housing 2. Home ownership
I. Series II. Firth, Lisa
363.5-dc22

ISBN-13: 978 1 86168 505 6

Printed in Great Britain
MWL Print Group Ltd

Cover
The illustration on the front cover is by
Simon Kneebone.

CONTENTS

Useful information for readers

Dear Reader,

Issues: The Housing Issue

Until recently, the housing market was enjoying a boom period, with property prices higher than ever before – however, the global financial crisis put an end to this. How has the crash affected the ordinary homeowner, as well as those looking to get onto the property ladder? Will the shortage of social housing now need to be addressed? How have mortgage providers dealt with the crisis? This title examines the issues.

The purpose of *Issues*

The Housing Issue is the one hundred and eighty-first volume in the **Issues** series. The aim of this series is to offer up-to-date information about important issues in our world. Whether you are a regular reader or new to the series, we do hope you find this book a useful overview of the many and complex issues involved in the topic.

Titles in the **Issues** series are resource books designed to be of especial use to those undertaking project work or requiring an overview of facts, opinions and information on a particular subject, particularly as a prelude to undertaking their own research.

The information in this book is not from a single author, publication or organisation; the value of this unique series lies in the fact that it presents information from a wide variety of sources, including:

⇨ Government reports and statistics
⇨ Newspaper articles and features
⇨ Information from think-tanks and policy institutes
⇨ Magazine features and surveys
⇨ Website material
⇨ Literature from lobby groups and charitable organisations. *

Critical evaluation

Because the information reprinted here is from a number of different sources, readers should bear in mind the origin of the text and whether the source is likely to have a particular bias or agenda when presenting information (just as they would if undertaking their own research). It is hoped that, as you read about the many aspects of the issues explored in this book, you will critically evaluate the information presented. It is important that you decide whether you are being presented with facts or opinions. Does the writer give a biased or an unbiased report? If an opinion is being expressed, do you agree with the writer?

The Housing Issue offers a useful starting point for those who need convenient access to information about the many issues involved. However, it is only a starting point. Following each article is a URL to the relevant organisation's website, which you may wish to visit for further information.

Kind regards,

Lisa Firth
Editor, **Issues** series

** Please note that Independence Publishers has no political affiliations or opinions on the topics covered in the **Issues** series, and any views quoted in this book are not necessarily those of the publisher or its staff.*

ISSUES TODAY
A RESOURCE FOR KEY STAGE 3

Younger readers can also benefit from the thorough editorial process which characterises the **Issues** series with our resource books for 11- to 14-year-old students, **Issues Today**. In addition to containing information from a wide range of sources, rewritten with this age group in mind, **Issues Today** titles also feature comprehensive glossaries, an accessible and attractive layout and handy tasks and assignments which can be used in class, for homework or as a revision aid. In addition, these titles are fully photocopiable. For more information, please visit our website (www.independence. co.uk).

First-time buyers wait to get on property ladder

First-time buyers who do not get help from their parents are having to save for longer to get on the property ladder, new figures suggest

The average age of first-time buyers who do not receive financial backing from relatives has risen sharply from 33 to 37 in the past two years.

The increase has been attributed to banks tightening their lending criteria amid the credit crunch, which has forced up the amount buyers must put down as a deposit.

> **The average age of first-time buyers who do not receive financial backing from relatives has risen sharply from 33 to 37 in the past two years**

As a result, around 80 per cent of young first-time buyers are seeking help from their parents to raise a deposit on a property, according to the Council of Mortgage Lenders (CML).

By Murray Wardrop

In its most recent monthly report, the CML said: 'Up until late 2007 – around the time the credit crunch began – the average age of first-time buyers excluding those getting help, was fairly stable at around 33.

'But since then, the average age has risen very sharply and now stands at around 37.

'Lending criteria have been scaled back to such an extent in the credit crunch that it has become exceptionally difficult for young people to get a mortgage without external help for a deposit.'

The figures show that although people without help from their parents are having to wait longer to buy a house, the average age of all first-time buyers has changed little since 2005 – at around 31.

However, recent CML research suggests that this has only been maintained because more people are turning to relatives for financial help towards deposits worth around 25 per cent of their property's value

Last month CML said that eight in ten first-time buyers under 30 had received parental support – the highest proportion on record.

When it last reported the figure in 2007, the CML said less than half this figure – 38 per cent – relied on their parents and others to help with their deposit.

However, the group has suggested this week that there are signs of banks and building societies slackening their lending criteria, offering hope to thousands of first-time buyers.

'In recent months lending criteria have begun to ease somewhat. It is likely that those young people not lucky enough to receive help from family, will not have to wait quite so long before getting a mortgage,' it said.

5 August 2009

The housing market and first-time buyers

Loans for house purchase and remortgage

	Number of house purchase loans	Value of house purchase loans (£m)	Number of remortgage loans	Value of remortgage loans (£m)
June 2009	45,000	5,900	34,000	4,200
Change from May 2009	+23%	+26%	+13%	+14%
Change from June 2008	-6%	-17%	-55%	-60%

First-time buyers, lending and affordability

	Number of loans	Value of loans (£m)	Average loan to value	Average income multiple	Proportion of income on interest payments
June 2009	17,200	1,900	75%	3.08	14.9%
Change from May 2009	+26%	+27%	75%	3.04	14.9%
Change from June 2008	-7%	-21%	87%	3.33	19.8%

Source: Council of Mortgage Lenders (CML), 11 August 2009.

Household projections to 2031, England

Information from the Department for Communities and Local Government

The latest national statistics on household projections to 2031 for England were released under the auspices of the UK Statistics Authority on 11 March 2009.

This statistical release presents national statistics on the projected number of households in England and its regions to 2031. The figures in this release are based on the 2006-based population projections and replace the 2004-based household projections released in February 2008.

The household projections are produced by applying projected household formation rates to the population projections published by the Office for National Statistics. The assumptions underlying national household and population projections are demographic trend based. They are not forecasts. They do not attempt to predict the impact that future government policies, changing economic circumstances or other factors might have on demographic behaviour. They provide the household levels and structures that would result if the assumptions based on previous demographic trends in the population and household formation rates were to be realised in practice.

Key points from the latest release are:

⇨ The number of households in England is projected to grow to 27.8 million in 2031, an increase of 6.3 million (29 per cent) over the 2006 estimate, or 252,000 households per year.

⇨ Population growth is the main driver of household growth, accounting for nearly three-quarters of the increase in households between 2006 and 2031.

⇨ One-person households are projected to increase by 163,000 per year, equating to two-thirds of the increase in households.

⇨ By 2031, 32 per cent of households will be headed by those aged 65 or over, up from 26 per cent in 2006.

⇨ By 2031, 18 per cent of the total population of England is projected to live alone, compared with 13 per cent in 2006.

⇨ The South East region has the largest absolute increase in households of 39,000 per year from 2006 to 2031, a 28 per cent rise from the 2006 level.

⇨ The North East region shows the smallest growth in households, at 8,300 per year from 2006 to 2031, or a 19 per cent rise from the 2006 level.

11 March 2009

⇨ The above information is reprinted with kind permission from the Department for Communities and Local Government. Visit www.communities.gov.uk for more information.

© Crown copyright

Home building

The facts

1. Britain is experiencing a housing crisis
Current home building levels are nowhere near enough to meet demand. Last year 160,000 new homes were built in England, compared with projected household growth of 223,000 per year.

2. The Government has raised home building targets
The Government has set a housing target of 240,000 homes per year by 2016, and a total of three million homes by 2020.

3. Britain's planning system is still not bringing land forward quickly enough to meet housing needs
It takes on average 15 months for home builders to receive full planning permission on sites they wish to develop. This excludes time taken for pre-application discussions, which can extend the whole process to over two years in many cases.

4. Britain's home builders are working hard to meet housing needs
New home completions have risen some 35% since 2001.

5. Home building does not pose a threat to the countryside
Green belt land comprises 13% of total land in England. Only 8% of land in the UK is classed as urban, half the figure in Holland and lower than Belgium, Denmark and Germany.

6. New homes are far more environmentally friendly and sustainable
Due to building standards introduced in 2006, new homes are now 40% more energy efficient than new homes built at the beginning of the decade.

⇨ The above information is reprinted with kind permission from the Home Builders Federation. Visit www.hbf.co.uk for more information.
© HBF

Rural residents face 280-year wait for a home

Information from Inside Housing

By Martin Hilditch

Residents in some areas of rural England would have to wait 280 years to be allocated a new home because so few new properties are being built, a study reveals.

People applying for an affordable home in the ten rural districts with the longest waiting lists would face a wait on average of up to 90 years

People applying for an affordable home in the ten rural districts with the longest waiting lists would face a wait on average of up to 90 years before enough new homes were built to clear the backlog, according to the National Housing Federation. It says East Riding of Yorkshire has a waiting list of 9,975 households – but with just 36 affordable homes built on average over the last three years it would take 280 years to provide everyone on the waiting list with a new-built home.

Newark and Sherwood, in Nottinghamshire, has a waiting list of 8,046 households – but only 44 homes have been built on average over the last three, resulting in a potential wait of 183 years for a new social home.

And people in Wychavon, Worcestershire, are looking at a wait of up to 87 years for their home – if the current rate of building new homes is maintained and no-one else is added to the waiting list.

Last year, three rural districts saw less than ten new affordable homes built – with four built in the Cotswold district, Gloucestershire, five in Alnwick, in Northumberland, and six in West Somerset.

The Federation's figures also show that the least affordable rural district is the Isles of Scilly, where the average house price is £335,000 compared to an average salary of £14,420, with a house price/salary ratio of 23.2.

The second least affordable rural district is Chichester, Sussex, where the average house price is £340,063 compared to an average salary of £16,463, with a house price/salary ratio of 20.7.

The new research also shows that second home ownership is a major issue in some of England's most attractive rural areas. The rural district with the highest proportion of second homes is the Isles of Scilly with 18.5 per cent. In South Hams, Devon, 9.83 per cent are second homes, and in North Cornwall 9.56 per cent are second homes.

The least affordable rural district is the Isles of Scilly, where the average house price is £335,000 compared to an average salary of £14,420

Federation chief executive David Orr said: 'So few affordable homes are being built in the English countryside that in some areas it will take 280 years to provide everyone on a waiting list with a new house.'
23 July 2009

⇨ The above information is reprinted with kind permission from Inside Housing. Visit www.insidehousing. co.uk for more information.

© Inside Housing

Nearly a third of young men live with their parents

Information from the Office for National Statistics

Nearly a third of men and a fifth of women aged 20 to 34 live with their parents, the Office for National Statistics reports today.

Figures published in the annual ONS 'state of the nation' report *Social Trends* show that, in the second quarter of 2008, 29 per cent of 20 to 34-year-old men and 18 per cent of women of the same age lived with their parents. This equated to around 1.8 million men and 1.1 million women.

In 2008 more than half (52 per cent) of men aged 20 to 24 and more than a third (37 per cent) of women lived with their parents

---

Social Trends, which this year takes the theme of households, families and children, also shows that the greatest proportion of this age group living with their parents was aged 20 to 24. In 2008 more than half (52 per cent) of men aged 20 to 24 and more than a third (37 per cent) of women lived with their parents.

Since 2001, the number of 20 to 34-year-olds living at the parental home has increased by nearly 300,000. In 2001, the proportion of young adults living at home stood at 27 per cent of 20 to 34-year-old men and 15 per cent of women in the same age group.

Part of the reason for the increase in the number of young people living with their parents may be that more young adults are continuing their studies after compulsory education.

Over the past four decades the number of students in higher education in the UK has quadrupled, rising from 621,000 in 1970/71 to more than 2.5 million in 2006/07.

Another factor may be that the unemployment rate is higher for people aged 16 to 24 than for older people.

In the second quarter of 2008, 20 per cent of 16 to 24-year-olds in the UK with dependent children and 13 per cent without dependent children were unemployed. This compares with six per cent of people with dependent children and four per cent of people without dependent children aged 25 to 34 and three per cent of people with and without dependent children aged between 50 and state pension age.

According to a Eurobarometer survey in 2007, the most common reasons given by young adults in Europe for why young people live with their parents were that they couldn't afford to move out or that there wasn't enough affordable housing available.

Supply of affordable housing

Trends in the gross supply of affordable housing by type of scheme, England, 1998-99 to 2007-08.

number of homes (y-axis: 0 to 60000)

- All affordable
- Social rent
- Low cost home ownership
- Intermediate affordable housing
- Intermediate rent

(x-axis: 1998-99, 1999-00, 2000-01, 2001-02, 2002-03, 2003-04, 2004-05, 2005-06, 2006-07, 2007-08)

In 2007-08, 29,370 affordable homes were social rent, of which:

- Section 106 nil grant total – 3,130
- Private Finance Initiative – 180
- Local authorities (new build) – 310
- Other Housing Corporation schemes – 660
- Housing Corporation (acquisitions) – 3,390
- Housing Corporation (new build) 21,700

In 2007-08, 23,250 affordable homes were low cost home ownership, of which:

- Assisted Purchase Schemes 2,460
- Section 106 nil grant total – 5,090
- Housing Corporation (new build) 12,040
- Housing Corporation (acquisitions) 3,390
- Other Housing Corporation schemes – 130

Source: Housing Corporation, English Partnerships, local authorities. Taken from the document 'Affordable housing supply, England, 2007-08' from the Dept. for Communities and Local Government. Crown copyright.

Around four in ten (38 per cent) people in the UK aged 15 to 30 believed that the main reason young adults lived with their parents was because they couldn't afford to move out and around four in ten (44 per cent) felt it was because of a lack of affordable housing.

Around four in ten (38 per cent) people in the UK aged 15 to 30 believed that the main reason young adults lived with their parents was because they couldn't afford to move out

---

For the EU-27 countries as a whole, a higher proportion of respondents (44 per cent) believed young adults couldn't afford to move out than in the UK but a smaller proportion (28 per cent) felt there was a lack of affordable housing.

Around one in eight (12 per cent) 15 to 30-year-olds in the UK felt the main reason young adults stayed at home was because they wanted the comforts at home without the responsibilities. In the EU-27 countries as a whole this figure was around one in six (16 per cent).

15 April 2009

⇨ The above information is reprinted with kind permission from the Office for National Statistics. Visit www.statistics.gov.uk for more information.

© Crown copyright

Brits have given up hope of ever owning a home

Almost 70% of first-time buyers think they will never get on the ladder

Almost seven in ten first-time buyers in the UK have given up hope of ever owning their own home, according to new research published by PropertyLive.co.uk, the UK's first regulated property website.

Despite falling house prices and record low interest rates, 65% of non-homeowners in the UK still believe that they will never have enough money to get on the property ladder.

Of those still living in hope, one in 20 (5%) think they will have to wait more than five years to get a mortgage. One in seven (14%) estimate they could be on the ladder in between two and five years' time, while one in ten (10%) think it will be between one and two years; and one in 20 (5%) in between six months and a year.

A regional breakdown of the figures (see chart below) found that:
⇨ First-time buyers in Norwich are the most pessimistic about their chances of buying a home, with 92% doubtful that they will ever have enough money to get a mortgage.
⇨ People in Sheffield are the most optimistic, with only 47% per cent of them believing they will never get on the property ladder.

Peter Bolton King, Chief Executive of the National Federation of Property Professionals (NFoPP), which regulates PropertyLive.co.uk, said: 'With banks still refusing to lend and the Government doing practically nothing to help first-time buyers, it's little wonder that so many people have given up hope of every owning their own home.

'First-time buyers are the bedrock of a healthy housing market. It's a real shame that Alastair Darling missed an opportunity to help them by extending the stamp duty holiday to the rest of the market and by scrapping Home Information Packs. In failing to do that he dashed the hopes of thousands of hard-working people who are saving in the hope of getting the keys to their own home.'

12 June 2009

⇨ The above information is reprinted with kind permission from PropertyLive.co.uk. Visit www.propertylive.co.uk for more information.

© PropertyLive.co.uk

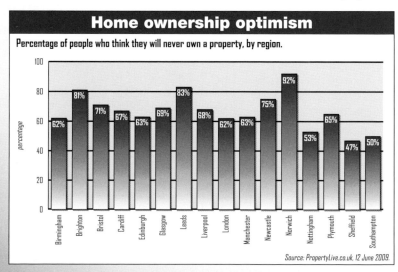

Affordable housing target will be missed

Government will miss affordable housing target, its own figures reveal. New home construction will fall more than 13,000 short of long-standing 70,000 target

By Kathryn Hopkins

The government is certain to break its long-standing promise to be building 70,000 affordable homes a year by 2010-11, the *Guardian* has learned.

As Gordon Brown unveiled his party's relaunch document, entitled *Building Britain's Future*, this week with a pledge to build more affordable homes over the next two years, a breakdown of the government's own figures shows that the housing target now falls short of plans outlined two years ago.

In 2007, the then housing minister Yvette Cooper pledged to provide more than 70,000 affordable homes a year by 2010-11. But detailed figures issued in a briefing this week show that the government is failing to meet its original target by at least 13,550 a year: it plans to deliver only 56,450 dwellings in 2010-11, after building 55,500 in 2009-10.

In a further change from its original programme for 2010-11, only 13,500 of the 56,450 homes will be council housing. Two years ago, the government said that 45,000 out of the 70,000 affordable homes promised would be for social renting.

A spokesperson for the Department of Communities and Local Government said: 'Our focus is on keeping affordable housing going in the current climate: that's why we're increasing investment, kick-starting new housing projects and protecting jobs. We know our long-term targets are extremely challenging right now, but we're determined to take the action necessary to build for Britain's recovery.'

Lord Oakeshott, the Liberal Democrats' Treasury spokesman, said: 'You couldn't make it up. We all knew that *Building Britain's Future* contained a string of re-announced targets, but this is something else – to

announce a lower target after you have failed and pretend it's progress. It's surreal. This is a real slap in the face to the three million people in desperate housing need on our council house waiting lists.'

Shadow housing minister Grant Shapps said: 'Gordon Brown's dog-whistle politics on British homes for British people can't disguise the fact that his government has failed to tackle the British housing crisis. After a succession of housing ministers and glossy reports, housebuilding is at its lowest level since 1947. Targets come, and targets go, exposing a continued failure to deliver.'

The Construction Products Association (CPA) has also discovered that despite the government building fewer houses, the programme will cost more money. The government said this week that an additional £1.5bn would be spent over the next two years

to deliver 20,000 new homes, which will be part of the approximate total of 110,000 affordable homes now being promised over the next two years.

Michael Ankers, chief executive of the CPA, said: 'It is difficult to understand why they need additional money to deliver fewer houses. The last comprehensive spending review allocated the necessary funds to deliver the government's programme to the end of 2010-11. So why do they now need to divert money from other capital programmes to deliver a lower target that should be costing less? It sounds very much like the government is promising less for more.'

He added that if the funds required for this housing were being reallocated from elsewhere, then the government would need to explain which other capital projects will not now go ahead. 'The sooner this is clarified, the better,' he said.

1 July 2009

© *Guardian News & Media Ltd 2009*

Profiting from repossession

A chance to buy at reasonable prices or making a profit out of others' misery?

Repossessed homes are big business and a new website gives investors the chance to snap them up. Rupert Jones reports.

A short cut to a bargain home, or a way of profiting from other people's misery? It is a debate that will rumble on after a new website was unveiled today that allows investors to snap up repossessed properties at competitive prices.

The launch of PropertyEarth comes three months after the arrival on these shores of controversial US 'repo' auction company REDC, which specialises in selling off homes seized by banks and building societies.

Repossession is clearly big business – and getting bigger. Last year 40,000 UK families and individuals were forced to hand their keys to their mortgage lender and, this week, leading economist Ian Shepherdson predicted repossessions will jump to between 100,000 and 120,000 per year by 2011, as levels of unemployment increase and people's incomes become squeezed.

Shepherdson's forecast was made at the Chartered Institute of Housing's annual conference in Harrogate.

But not everyone shares this super-gloomy view. The Council of Mortgage Lenders had predicted 75,000 repossessions this year, but said recently that this now 'looks pessimistic'. The CML is expected to revise this figure downwards next week.

Launched today, PropertyEarth describes itself as a one-stop search engine which aims to match up investor landlords and other buyers with 'chain-free' properties.

Many of these are homes repossessed by mortgage lenders after the people living there got into financial difficulties. Others are newly built properties that developers have failed to sell, and previously owned homes that housebuilders have ended up being stuck with after running part-exchange schemes.

What makes the website appealing for buyers, claim those behind it, is that in all cases the lender or developer is looking for a quick sale, so the properties tend to be priced to reflect that. This week there were several hundred listed on the site, ranging from a one-bedroom ground floor flat in Bolton costing £19,950 to a four-bed detached house located within an 'exclusive gated area' in picturesque West Malling, Kent, with a £550,000 price-tag.

PropertyEarth founder Dominic Toller says his site 'gives the consumer one place to go to find those chain-free properties' – particularly 'distressed sale' properties. He is targeting professional buy-to-let investors but says first- and second-time buyers may also want to use it to search for a suitable home. The site makes its money by charging sellers a marketing fee.

But Toller rejects any suggestion that his firm is profiting from others' misfortune, describing PropertyEarth as 'a consumer champion'. He adds: 'If we do our job, we'll help that property get sold more quickly and for more money.'

His website is not the first to plough this particular furrow. Whitehot Property also specialises in selling repossessed and part-exchange properties. This week it was listing 859 homes, with prices starting from £38,950 for a two-bedroom mid-terrace house in an old mining village close to Bishop Auckland in County Durham, rising all the way to £1.65m for 16th-century Earls Croome Court in Worcestershire, the former seat of the Earl of Coventry, which must rank as one of Britain's most expensive 'repos'.

According to a report in *Country Life*, the owners of the seven-bedroom country house failed to keep up with their mortgage payments and it ended up being repossessed. Last year it was on sale with a guide price of £1.95m.

Whitehot Property says the homes on its site can be 'perfect' for first-time buyers (well, perhaps not Earls Croome Court) because 'they are realistically priced to sell, not to make vast profits for the sellers'.

Last year 40,000 UK families and individuals were forced to hand their keys to their mortgage lender

Also, you are buying directly from a lender or housebuilder, so there is no chain to worry about. And many properties come with additional incentives such as the stamp duty or legal fees paid. While selling off repossessed homes in this way might seem unpalatable to some, websites such as these arguably help mortgage lenders comply with rules requiring them to get the best possible price for these properties on behalf of their borrowers.

Alternatively, you could take the view that labelling a property a repossession pushes down the likely sale price, and also has an impact on neighbouring homes.

PropertyEarth and Whitehot Property are competing with California-based repossessions specialist REDC, which opened for business in Britain earlier this year and held its first auctions at the end of March. REDC's next two auctions take place in Manchester on 27 June and central London on 28 June.

Earlier this year, we told how REDC had raised hackles among some first-time buyers and estate agents, in part because of the whopping 10% buyer's fee that successful bidders must hand over to the auction company.

20 June 2009

Social housing waiting lists 'growing'

One in ten people will be on a social housing waiting list by 2020, National Housing Federation warns

Around 6.5m people – or one in ten of the population – will be on social housing waiting lists in England by 2020 unless urgent action is taken, according to new figures.

The National Housing Federation says that if current trends continue the total number of people waiting for an affordable home will be 2m more than when the Government announced, in July 2007, that it would build 3m homes by 2020 in order to slash waiting lists.

'To get house-building back on track we need an urgent affordable house building programme, through which housing associations can quickly deliver thousands of decent homes'

Ministers announced their ambitious house-building plans two years ago, in an effort to tackle the nation's housing crisis by increasing the number of new homes being built – with a plan to escalate the number of new homes delivered each year to 240,000 by 2016.

However, because of the meltdown in private sector house-building, following the economic downturn, the number of new homes being built has slumped to around 70,000 per year – while the number of people on waiting lists is continuing to soar.

With the effect of the recession and repossessions making the need for social housing even greater, the Federation, which represents England's housing associations, believes that ministers should try to ensure a minimum of 50,000 new social homes are delivered over the next year.

Housing associations are currently the only organisations still building affordable housing in volume and have delivered around half of all new homes this year.

Under the Federation's proposals, which are with the Prime Minister and Communities Secretary for their consideration, housing associations would deliver thousands of new social homes through £3.2bn of public investment. One in four of the new homes built under the plan would be funded by housing associations at no cost to the taxpayer.

As well as delivering new homes, the Federation's proposed house-building drive would pump desperately needed funds into many deprived areas, help boost the construction industry, avoid serious skills shortages and stimulate long-term market stability.

Federation chief executive David Orr said: 'It is deeply disturbing that, if current trends continue, one in ten of the population would be on waiting lists by 2020.

'The Government was right two years ago to set a target of building 3m homes by 2020, but the programme has been severely dented by the impact of the recession – which has sent the private house-building sector from boom to bust.

'To get house-building back on track we need an urgent affordable house-building programme, through which housing associations can quickly deliver thousands of decent homes for social rent.

'If ministers invest £3.2bn, housing associations will complement this with their own investment, and deliver 50,000 new social homes by next June.

'The housing association sector is continuing to build through the recession and is uniquely placed to deliver thousands of new homes over the next 12 months. One in four of these homes would be funded directly by housing associations and wouldn't cost taxpayers a penny.

'This would be an excellent springboard from which to get the house-building programme back on track.'
17 June 2009

⇨ The above information is reprinted with kind permission from the National Housing Federation. Visit www.housing.org.uk for more information.

© National Housing Federation

Growing up in social housing in Britain

A profile of four generations from 1946 to the present day – summary report

This research draws on four British birth cohort studies to examine the role of social housing for four generations of families since the Second World War. It describes how housing for families changed over time, and explores the relationship between social housing, family circumstances, and experiences for the children when they reached adulthood.

Key findings

⇨ Four generations ago, families in social housing included almost the full social range. Council and housing association homes offered high quality. However, from the 1960s, home ownership took over from social housing as the main type of housing for families. Over time, the more advantaged families moved out. Increasingly, encouraged by policy, social housing has acted as a 'safety net'. It has also lost out in term of relative desirability;

⇨ Society is also now more unequal than it was. The result is that the gap between the socioeconomic circumstances of children in social housing and other tenures is wider than for any previous generation;

⇨ On average, those who lived in social housing as children were worse off as adults in terms of health, well-being, education and employment than their peers;

⇨ Most of this pattern, especially for people born in 1946, can be explained by differences in family background. However, for people born in 1958 and more so in 1970, living in social housing as a child was still associated with some worse adult outcomes, even after accounting for family background;

⇨ These patterns are stronger for women than men. They do not vary substantially by social class, region, housing quality or neighbourhood characteristics. They suggest that as the social housing sector has become smaller and more focused on the most disadvantaged, it has become less likely to deliver positive benefits in other aspects of people's lives;

⇨ Recent policy statements have proposed reducing the security of tenure of social tenants or requiring them to seek work. This report offers no support for reducing the attractiveness of social renting or the number of homes available. If anything, it suggests the reverse: we need to help social housing catch up with the desirability of home-ownership housing, and increase its social mix. Crucially, other areas of social policy, such as childcare and education, also need to more effectively tackle childhood tenure gaps as these cannot be effectively addressed through housing policy initiatives.

The study

This research builds on an earlier study by many of the same team, *The Public Value of Social Housing* (Feinstein et al, 2008). It aims to illuminate the relationship between housing in childhood and people's experiences in adulthood, and thus to inform current policy debate on the future of social housing and its role in tackling social exclusion and promoting greater equality and social mobility.

The report uses data from four British cohort studies, which have traced large samples of people born in 1946, 1958, 1970 and 2000 with regular and wide-ranging interviews throughout their lives. Using this data enables us to examine changes over individual lifetimes, including the relationship between childhood housing experiences and a wide range of later outcomes in the domains of health, well-being, education, income and employment. It also enables us to compare the experiences of people in different generations, under different socio-economic conditions and policy regimes. We focus on the situation of families with children.

Growing up in social housing

Evidence from the cohort studies confirms the important role social housing has played in post-war British childhoods. Families with children have always been over-represented in social housing compared to other households. However, both the proportion of families in social housing and their over-representation compared to other households have diminished over time, as home ownership increased. Only 21% of the children born in the 2000 cohort were in social housing at age five, compared to 37% born in 1946 at a similar age. Far fewer of today's children are experiencing social housing than previous generations.

After the war, most people who came into social housing came from the private rented sector. Social housing acted as a 'step up' in quality.

Over time, growing shares came from home ownership, and here social housing was acting more as a 'safety net', perhaps after family breakdown or repossession. Over 70% of those born in 1958 and 1970 who moved out of social housing in childhood moved into home ownership, demonstrating how social housing was also acting as a 'stepping stone' to a tenure that was widely seen as more desirable than any form of renting.

Social housing and increasing concentrations of disadvantage

As the role of social housing changed for families, so its tenants became increasingly disadvantaged. When the 1946 cohort were aged four, 11% of the best-off fifth of families were in social housing, compared to 27% of the least well-off. By the time the 2000 cohort were aged five, the tenure gap had grown hugely: just 2% of the best-off fifth were in social housing while 49% of the least well-off were.

The richness of the cohort studies reveals how social housing populations changed in many other ways, especially after 1970. For example, for children in home ownership, the proportion born to a single mother was unchanged between 1970 and 2000, while the proportion in social housing grew from 6% to 28%. Mothers of those born in 1958 were more likely to work when their children were of pre-school age if they were social renters than if they were homeowners. For the 1970 cohort there was little difference by the kind of tenure that their parents lived in, and by the time the 2000 cohort were aged five, the home owner mothers were twice as likely to be working as the social tenant mothers. This reflects transition in mothers' economic activity over time: from working class necessity to middle class norm, and is an example of how wide-ranging social changes affected children and the housing system.

Social housing also began to lose out to other tenures in terms of quality and desirability as measured by living in flats, overcrowding and lack of facilities. No more than 11% of children born in 1946 in social housing experienced living in flats (a less desirable housing type

for families), overcrowding, lack of bathroom or hot water – while for those whose parents were home owners the figure was 20%. For those whose parents were private tenants, a massive 66% experienced at least one of these less desirable features. By the 1958 cohort, home ownership had overtaken social housing in the quality stakes, and by the 2000 cohort at least 20% of children in social housing experienced one of these less desirable features (mainly living in flats), and social housing was in third place behind owning and private renting.

Thus, over successive generations, children growing up in social housing experienced several cumulative processes of disadvantage:
⇨ as individuals, they were more likely to come from disadvantaged families;
⇨ given the increasing disadvantage of social renting households generally, they were more likely to be surrounded by disadvantaged neighbours;
⇨ on the measures we have used, their homes were more likely to fall short in quality and desirability in absolute terms and relative to other tenures.

There is now a much bigger tenure divide among today's children than any other post-war generation.

Social housing in childhood and adult outcomes

For the three earlier cohorts, who have now moved into adulthood, we examined whether there was a relationship between their childhood tenure and adult outcomes in five areas: health and health-related behaviours, well-being, education, employment, and income. Did being in social housing as a child have any long-term implications?

For each generation and every measure we used, those who had ever been in social housing in childhood fared worse as adults. For example, at age 34 in 2004, those born in 1970 who had ever been in social housing in childhood rated their health at an average score of 2.92 out of four, while those who had never been in social housing in childhood rated their health at 3.13 out of four. 79% of the 'ever' group were in paid

employment, while 86% of the 'never' group were.

However, this is partly due to the background characteristics of individuals who end up in different tenures. We attempted to isolate tenure by controlling for factors that might influence tenure position or outcomes. These included, for example, parents' education, occupation, income and interest in education, teachers' rating of child's progress, whether the child was bullied, how happy the child was, whether they wet the bed, their height and weight, and for the 1958 and 1970 cohorts, characteristics of their schools.

After applying these controls, we found that there were no long-term associations between childhood social housing and most adult outcomes for the 1946 cohort. This shows that social housing has no inherent negative consequences.

However, more statistically significant associations do remain even after controls for the 1958 and 1970 cohorts in every domain, although not for every indicator, and not at every age. For example, about half of the gap between the group who were 'ever in social housing in childhood' and those 'never in social housing in childhood' that had been found on measures of self-assessed health, cigarettes smoked and paid employment remained after controlling for background factors. Notably, we did not find any situations where the 'ever' group had more positive scores than their counterparts.

Thus there is no evidence of social housing appearing to counteract earlier disadvantage with positive, 'value added' effects on adult out-comes. Effect sizes are typically larger for the 1970 cohort than for the 1958 cohort, indicating a widening gap over time.

Potential explanations

We proposed and tested a number of possible explanations for the link between childhood housing tenure and later adult outcomes.

We found that there were no substantial differences between regions, despite the different size of the social housing sector in different regions. Nor did we find that the quality of housing (based on overcrowding and amenities) made a difference to the strength of the associations. These results are surprising. They suggest that, even after the inclusion of many controls, 'tenure' may still be capturing background character-istics of people in different tenures.

One theory is that social housing is associated with worse outcomes because of the characteristics of the neighbourhoods in which it is located. We could only explore this for the 1958 cohort at ages 16 and 23, using data for census enumeration districts. We found that neither the level of unemployment nor the level of social housing in a neighbourhood seemed to explain the relationship between childhood housing tenure and adult outcomes, once added after other controls. Note that we inves-tigate neighbourhood characteristics in childhood. It is possible that neighbourhood characteristics ex-perienced in adulthood might be more influential.

We did find gender differences. For all cohorts, there were more and stronger statistically significant associations between childhood social housing and experiences in adulthood for women than for men. One explanation for this may lie in the different pathways followed in young adulthood by men and women who have grown up in social housing. For the 1958 and 1970 cohorts, we examined the ages at which young people first moved into independent living, formed their first partnership, and had their first child. We found tenure differences, even after controlling for level of parental advantage. Young people from social housing formed partnerships and became parents earlier than their similarly advantaged counterparts in other tenures, and this was particularly the case for women. These patterns became more marked over time. This suggests that there is an important role for interventions to support people's transitions into early adulthood, and a need for further research on how tenure may affect transitions.

We also found that negative associations with social housing were greater for people who moved into social housing in childhood than those who were in social housing but moved out. This indicates that the circumstances in which people enter social housing, not just the tenure itself, may be driving later outcomes.

Policy implications

One important contribution of this research is that it shows how difficult it is to identify 'tenure effects', where tenure means the ownership of property and the conditions on which it is held. Even with rich data and extensive controls it is hard to isolate tenure from the characteristics of the people in particular tenures, or from the wider bundles of characteristics with which particular tenures might be associated but which are not inherent to any particular tenure (factors like location, area characteristics, cost, quality and status).

This means that we should not make a leap from findings like this, which seem to show an association between particular tenures and particular outcomes, to very specific policies, such as changing tenancy conditions. We simply cannot tell whether detailed changes like this would have an influence on other public policy outcomes. Such interventions would need properly controlled evaluation to determine their value.

The research also provides a stock-take of post-war social housing. While it may be seen as disappointing that there appear to have been no discernible long-term benefits from the stability and low rents that social housing provided for families with children, our research also shows that social housing has been very successful when measured against some of its original objectives, including combating squalor and overcrowding. The findings show social housing not failing but in transition – originally establishing better housing conditions and providing the security and affordability not available elsewhere in the system, but moving from this role to a 'safety net' role as other aspects of the housing system evolved.

So what should we expect housing policy to do now? Clearly a return to a post-war housing system is neither possible nor desirable, but our work does suggest that if we expect social housing not to compound disadvantage, and perhaps to help, we would have a better chance if the sector had broader appeal and greater relative advantages. This would require a cross-tenure approach in order to shift housing preferences, demand and need. A 'progressive vision' of social housing's role must be a wide one.

The gap between the socioeconomic circumstances of children in social housing and other tenures is now wider than for any previous generation

---

It is also crucial to recognise the role of wider social policies aimed at tackling poverty and disadvantage. Social housing policy alone can have limited effect. The shrinkage of the social housing sector and the increasing concentration of disadvantage within it has come about because of wider housing policies to support home ownership and as a result of broader social and economic changes, as well as through social housing policy. Social housing, like other parts of the welfare state, has to run harder to stand still in the face of growing social inequality, and has in practice become less able to promote positive life chances in these circumstances. The more that we target social housing on the disadvantaged, the less can be expected of specific housing policies (for example, changes in tenancy conditions). In some respects we might expect other social policies targeted towards those who need social housing to do far more, and housing policy to do less, to ensure that the disadvantage with which people enter the social housing sector does not continue or get worse.
18 June 2009

⇨ The above information is reprinted with kind permission from the Tenant Services Authority. Visit www.tenantservicesauthority.org for more information.
© *Tenant Services Authority*

Who's living in my social housing?

Information from Straight Statistics

The rise of the British National Party has been attributed in part to claims that immigrants are getting favourable access to social housing. The Equality and Human Rights Commission set out to investigate the claims, and concluded that they are a myth.

Less than two per cent of the occupants of council houses or housing association homes arrived in Britain in the past five years. New immigrants are far more likely to be found in privately-rented accommodation.

But not all the newspapers chose to read the Commission's report that way. The *Daily Mail*, *Daily Express* and *Daily Star* went for a different angle. 'One in 10 Council Homes to Migrants' huffed the *Star*. The *Mail* took the same line. Nowhere in either story was the Commission's 'top line' – that only 1.8 per cent of social housing had gone to immigrants who arrived in the UK in the past five years. Here's how the *Mail* headlined the story: 'Immigrants take 10% of state housing'.

The *Daily Telegraph*, *Independent*, and *Daily Mirror* might have been reading a different report. 'Immigrants "don't jump homes list"' said the *Mirror*, the quotes in the headline indicating that this was a claim made by somebody else. The *Telegraph* also resorted to quotes in its headline, around the word myth. However, all three papers did focus on the top line finding of the study, carried out for the commission by the Institute for Public Policy Research. Here's how the *Telegraph* reported it: 'The 'myth' that immigrants jump the social housing queue'.

So who's right? Both these points are made in the report, so nobody's actually lying. But the claim the *Mail*, *Express* and *Star* chose to focus on is fairly irrelevant to the debate. It is

that ten per cent of social housing is occupied by people who were not born in the UK. There are four million social homes, so the papers explained that meant 400,000 (a nice big number) were occupied by people not born in the UK – immigrants, in other words.

Except that many of these immigrants have been here for decades. They include elderly people of Asian or Caribbean origin who have lived here since the 1950s and 60s, worked hard, paid their taxes and are absolutely entitled to social housing. They were immigrants when they arrived but are such no longer. By implying that recent immigrants were occupying 400,000 homes the *Mail*, *Star* and *Express* misrepresented the findings.

So why do so many people believe what the report characterises as a myth? Partly it's because even a report showing that it is a myth can be reported in a way to suggest it is true. But partly it is also a matter of geography and of misperception. There are places, especially in London, where there are concentrations of recent immigrants in social housing. There are also quite a lot occupying homes that were council houses or flats, but were bought by their tenants and have subsequently become privately-rented accommodation. These homes are often misperceived by local residents as 'social housing', which they ceased to be some time ago.

The Home Office has also contributed by housing asylum seekers

in empty social housing around the country, the report acknowledges.

So if it is a myth, why has the Government announced plans to allow local authorities to give priority to local people? They seem already to be doing so, if the commission and the IPPR are right. It sounds as if the Government also believes the myth, or hasn't bothered to establish the facts first. No surprise there, then.
8 July 2009

⇨ The above information is reprinted with kind permission from Straight Statistics. Visit www.straightstatistics.org for more information.

© *Straight Statistics*

What's that?

I cut all the misleading items from the newspaper and this is all I've got left!

A third of households with children live in poor housing

Information from the Office for National Statistics

Nearly a third of households with children in England live in poor housing, nearly a third of children are classed as overweight or obese, and around a quarter of young people have been a victim of personal crime.

But fewer children are now living in low-income households and more children are taking part in school sports.

Figures published today in the Office for National Statistics publication *Social Trends* provide a picture of modern life for youngsters in the UK.

The annual publication, which this year has the theme of households, families and children, shows that many children are experiencing poor housing, health or well-being.

For example, nearly a third (31 per cent) of all households with dependent children in England in 2006 were found to be living in 'non-decent' homes that do not meet sufficient standards of upkeep, facilities, insulation and heating.

The figures also show an increasing proportion of children who are classified as either overweight or obese. In 2007, nearly a third of two to 15-year-olds in England (31 per cent of boys and 30 per cent of girls) were said to be overweight or obese.

In addition, the number of children counselled by ChildLine in the UK has increased substantially. In particular, the number of boys who contacted ChildLine more than doubled from 24,115 calls and letters in 1997/98 to 58,311 in 2007/08, increasing from 21 per cent of all contacts to 33 per cent.

The figures also show that one in four young people have been a victim of personal crime and that children are the highest risk group for pedestrian and cycling accidents.

Around a quarter (26 per cent) of ten to 25-year-olds in England and Wales were victims of some kind of personal crime over a 12-month period between 2005 and 2006. Within this age group, nearly two-fifths (38 per cent) of ten to 15-year-old boys were victims of personal crime.

And the figures indicate that in 2007, children in Great Britain under the age of 16 represented nearly a third (32 per cent) of all pedestrian casualties and over a fifth (22 per cent) of cycling casualties.

Other figures published today in *Social Trends* give details on children in low-income households as well as statistics on sports and other activities in which young people participate.

The proportion of children in the UK living in households with a disposable income well below the national average (below 60 per cent of median household disposable income) has fallen from a peak of 26 per cent in 1998/99 and 1999/2000 to 22 per cent in 2006/07.

The statistics also show that 90 per cent of pupils in England took part in at least two hours or more of physical education and out-of-hours school sport each week during term time in 2007/08. This is an increase of 21 percentage points since 2004/05.

Children today are more technologically minded than ever before. In 2007, nearly half (49 per cent) of all those aged eight to 17 in the UK who use the Internet had a page or profile on a social networking site. And 16 to 19-year-olds were the only group of all age groups to say that of all media activity they would miss their mobile phone the most.

However, traditional activities haven't been abandoned in favour of new technology. In 2007, 69 per cent of children aged nine and 59 per cent of children aged 11 in England said they enjoyed reading.
15 April 2009

⇨ The above information is reprinted with kind permission from the Office for National Statistics. Visit www.statistics.gov.uk for more information.

© Crown copyright

One million children overcrowded

Information from Shelter

Over one million children are now trapped in overcrowded housing, a rise of 54,000 in the last two years, Shelter has revealed today.

We are highlighting these new figures from the Survey of English Housing to urge the government to provide more affordable family-sized homes. This would help lift these children out of cramped conditions and end overcrowding for the next generation.

Living in confined conditions has a devastating effect on family life, especially children's safety and general health. Children in overcrowded housing are up to ten times more likely to contract meningitis than children in general.

The current legal definition of overcrowding, which remains unchanged since 1935, does not count children under one-year-old as a person living in the property and considers kitchens and living rooms as acceptable places to sleep. Under the current legal standard, a family of four living in a one-bedroom flat would not be classed as living in overcrowded accommodation.

There are already thousands of overcrowded families on the local authority housing waiting lists, in desperate need of an affordable family-sized home. Even more worryingly, recent Local Government Association estimates predict waiting lists will rise to top two million by 2011.

Sam Younger, Shelter's Chief Executive, said: 'For too long the issue of children living in overcrowded housing has been a hidden problem.

'There is no doubt that over-crowding has a massive impact on children's health, safety and future prospects and can cause depression for parents struggling to cope in cramped conditions. With many children unable to study due to a lack of space, the impact of overcrowding is robbing them of an education and a fair chance in life.

'Government must ensure enough affordable family-sized homes are built and introduce an updated definition of overcrowding that reflects a modern need for space and privacy.'

Jacqueline Pennant lives in a small two-bedroom house in Wandsworth, with her three children. Due to her cramped conditions her daughter sleeps in her bed and her younger son sleeps on a make-shift bed on the floor of her bedroom.

She says: 'My youngest has chronic asthma, which is made worse by sleeping so low to the ground and he has been in hospital a few times with the condition.

'My daughter shares a bed with me, which is not only inappropriate at her age, but incredibly painful for me. We can't carry on living in these conditions, my children are growing up fast and this is no way for them to live. I am so worried about the future.'
29 July 2009

⇨ The above information is reprinted with kind permission from Shelter. Visit www.shelter.org.uk for more information.

© Shelter

Attitudes to social housing

By Crispin Dowler

The government has published the research that informed its plans to allow councils to give priority to applicants with jobs.

A survey by polling company Ipsos MORI in 2008 found that 48 per cent of respondents believed more low-income working households should be given social homes, in preference to always housing the most vulnerable first.

The same proportion believed that people who had lived in an area for a long time should have priority for social housing.

But the message from focus groups, carried out for the Communities and Local Government department among people from low-income households across all tenures, presented a more nuanced picture.

The researchers reported that the focus groups illustrated the difficulties encountered when applying general beliefs and attitudes about social housing allocation to decisions about individual households in need.

Whilst participants supported notions of mixed communities, when presented with limited available stock, they reverted to allocating homes to the most explicitly vulnerable with the greatest immediate need.

On Friday the CLG launched a consultation on its plans to drop the 'cumulative preference' rule, which requires council allocations to prioritise those who fit more than one category of greatest housing need. The consultation, along with both survey reports on attitudes to housing, can be found at www.communities.gov.uk
3 August 2009

⇨ The above information is reprinted with kind permission from Inside Housing. Visit www.insidehousing.co.uk for more information.

© Inside Housing

New homes 'too small for everyday life'

Information from the Commission for Architecture and the Built Environment (CABE)

New homes are failing to provide enough space for everyday activities, according to new research conducted with the owners of 2,500 private new homes.

The findings, published in CABE's *Space in new homes: what residents think*, revealed that private homes do not provide enough space to prepare food easily, have friends round for dinner or find a quiet place to relax. All of the residents surveyed lived in homes that had been built between 2003 and 2006 and they included flats, houses and bungalows.

The findings showed that in all households:

⇨ 44 per cent said that there wasn't enough space for small children to play safely in the kitchen while meals are being prepared;

- WE NEED A THINNER TOASTER...

⇨ 47 per cent don't have enough space for all the furniture they have, or would like to have;

⇨ 35 per cent said they didn't have enough kitchen space for the appliances they need, such as a toaster or a microwave;

⇨ 37 per cent said they or their children do not have enough space to entertain guests privately;

Private homes do not provide enough space to prepare food easily, have friends round for dinner or find a quiet place to relax

---

⇨ 57 per cent don't have enough storage; and

⇨ 72 per cent said they did not have enough space for the three small bins required to recycle properly.

In fully occupied properties the situation is worse – for instance, 58 per cent don't have enough space for all the furniture they have, or would like to have. A fully occupied home is one where the number of bed spaces matches the number of inhabitants aged ten or over. A single bedroom counts as one bed space and double bed as two. The fact that 90 per cent of the homes surveyed had a spare bedroom adds extra weight to this research.

The research points to lower-income households suffering from more of the problems associated with a lack of space than wealthier households. This in turn may impact upon health and educational attainment.

Richard Simmons, CABE chief executive, comments: 'This research brings into question the argument that the market will meet the demands of people living in private housing developments. We need local planning authorities to ensure much higher space standards before giving developments the go-ahead.'

CABE believes that the implications of these findings are wide-reaching. Increased space in homes has direct implications for national policy priorities such as health and well-being, education and recycling. For example, dining as a family could encourage healthier eating habits and stronger family relationships. Children without space to entertain friends will do so outside the home, beyond parental supervision. Privacy at home is vital too – there are links between lack of space and mental health and well-being.

The government's 2007 Waste Strategy for England includes a target for 40 per cent of household waste to be recycled by 2010. Without the space for waste separation such targets will be very hard to meet.

CABE recommends that local authorities should use their existing powers to only approve developments that include sufficient space in new homes. CABE also believes that private housebuilders and estate agents should provide better information for buyers about space, using net floor area rather than the number of rooms; and that the Homes and Communities Agency should seize the opportunity to produce new cross-agency standards for space.
11 August 2009

⇨ The above information is reprinted with kind permission from CABE (Commission for Architecture and the Built Environment), The government's advisor on architecture, urban design and public space. Visit www.cabe.org.uk for more.
© CABE (*Commission for Architecture and the Built Environment*)

Your rights as a tenant

Is your landlord turning up unexpectedly and then threatening you with eviction because they don't like the type of music you listen to? Know your rights and put them in their place

Once you have entered into a contract, you have a number of rights under several statutes (The Housing Act 1988; The Family Law Act 1996; the Landlord and Tenant Act 1985 and The Protection From Eviction Act 1977).

Under these laws, your landlord cannot:

⇨ Turn up uninvited. Reasonable notice is required.

⇨ Neglect the place you rent.

⇨ Threaten you to leave, or offer money to vacate the premises.

⇨ Shut down utility supplies like gas, water or electricity.

⇨ Allow other tenants to threaten you.

⇨ Prevent your friends from visiting.

If you find yourself in a situation where you're having serious problems with your landlord, your local council has the power to prosecute them under The Landlord and Tenant Act 1985.

THE LANDLORD WANTS US OUT... APPARENTLY WE'RE TOO TIDY!

Housing officers from your council may also be able to help you if your utilities are cut off because of your landlord, or if you are being subjected to harassment or unlawful eviction.

As a tenant, you have the right to adequate living facilities such as hot and cold water, heating, electricity, ventilation, toilet facilities and a drainage system. If the house you are in does not meet health and safety standards you may be able to take legal action.

At the same time, your landlord has these grounds for eviction:

Mandatory eviction

The owner of the house wishes to come back and live in the property. The owner has gone bankrupt and the house is being repossessed. You are more than two months in arrears with your rent. You refuse or delay vital maintenance work to the building.

Discretionary eviction

A landlord can ask the court to decide if eviction is necessary if: you've broken the terms of your contract (i.e. trashed the place); you're consistently late in paying the rent; you lied about yourself to get the place; you're unemployed (in cases where having a job was a condition of the contract).

Your rights as a lodger

When you live in the same accommodation as your landlord, be it private or a B&B, your rights are often greatly reduced. They generally depend upon what you have agreed with your landlord. They do not have to apply for a court order to evict you, and the notice period can be as little as seven days. When living as a lodger you do not need to have a written agreement for the terms of your stay at the property, however it is probably wise to protect you from misunderstandings in the future.

This agreement should include:

⇨ How much rent you need to pay and when you should pay it;

⇨ How much notice you will be given if the rent is to be increased;

⇨ How much notice you have to give before moving out;

⇨ What services are provided and which you have to pay for, for example meals and laundry;

⇨ Whether you can have guests in your room and if there are restrictions on how long they can stay;

⇨ If your room is exclusively yours and if you can lock it;

⇨ If you have to pay a deposit for the room and if it's returnable on terminating your stay.

Your rights as a council tenant

If your council runs an introductory tenancy scheme it has the power to evict you before the 12-month period or extend the scheme for a further six months.

As a secure council tenant:

⇨ You can live in your home for the rest of your life as long as you follow the tenancy agreement;

⇨ You can buy your home at a discount and pass it onto someone in your family when you die;

⇨ You can take in lodgers and sub-let part of your home;

⇨ Repairs are done at no cost to you;

⇨ You are allowed to make improvements to your home and be paid for certain improvements if you move;

⇨ You can help to manage your estate;

⇨ You can exchange your property for another one;

⇨ You can be consulted on housing management matters.

⇨ The above information is reprinted with kind permission from TheSite. Visit www.thesite.org for more information on this and other related topics.

© TheSite

Research reveals Britain's 'reluctant landlords'

Frustrated sellers are turning to the lettings market, creating a glut of inexperienced landlords, according to the Association of Residential Lettings Agents (ARLA)

94 per cent of lettings agent respondents to the ARLA Members' Survey of the Private Rented Sector reported an increase of property coming onto the rental market because it could not be sold. ARLA's members believe that these figures confirm a trend that has been much discussed but thus far unproven other than through anecdotal evidence.

> **94 per cent of lettings agent respondents to the ARLA Members' Survey of the Private Rented Sector reported an increase of property coming onto the rental market because it could not be sold**

The trend was reported country-wide with even 92.2 per cent of landlords in 'prime' Central London locations reporting an upsurge in rentals coming onto the market for January, February and March.

Ian Potter, Operations Manager of ARLA, said: 'Sellers have been left with little option but to resort to renting out their property. These reluctant landlords need to understand the obligations of a landlord to their tenants, and the need to choose a regulated and qualified letting agent.'

Semi-detached houses appear to be the most common type of property succumbing to reluctant letting: UK-wide, 68 per cent of the agents surveyed saw an increase in the supply of these properties onto the rental market. This was followed by detached houses (67 per cent), terraced houses

Association of Residential Letting Agents

(52 per cent), with flats (29 per cent) and studios (11 per cent).

Ian Potter explained: 'These figures confirm the trends we have been hearing from ARLA's members that sellers looking to downsize are turning to the lettings market after being unable to sell.

'Detached and semi-detached houses are always traditionally harder to rent, but in this market there is now a glut of un-sellable properties coming onto the market. It is another sad indication of the work that the Government must take to free up the sales market and the need to regulate a lettings market that is becoming increasingly competitive.

'For those landlords new to renting, it's crucial that they look for a local lettings agent who is both regulated and abides by a code of practice. The agent will also have received the necessary training and qualifications, and consumers can be confident that any funds being held by them on your behalf are protected under client money protection schemes.'

According to ARLA's members, the increase in new landlords has led to tenants taking extra measures to gain assurances on the security of the property.

According to Lucy Morton, managing partner and head of lettings at W A Ellis, and president-elect of ARLA, there is a growing trend for tenants to be asking for references on landlords. She explained: 'Tenants are increasingly nervous about the security of landlords, we are also seeing tenants asking for assurances that the landlord will be able to cover his mortgage payments throughout their tenancy.'
8 April 2009

⇨ The above information is reprinted with kind permission from the Association of Residential Letting Agents (ARLA). Visit www.arla.co.uk for more information.
© Association of Residential Letting Agents (ARLA)

Student accommodation

What housing options are there for those entering Higher Education?

Halls of Residence

Most universities will be able to offer accommodation on campus. There are often limited places, and rooms in halls may be restricted to certain groups of students – for example, undergraduates and finalists. Most students will have to look for an alternative to staying in halls at some point in their university career.

It is advisable to contact your institution well in advance of starting your course to find out if they will have accommodation for you. If the answer is no, you will then have plenty of time to make alternative arrangements.

Most students will choose to live in halls if the option is available to them, but a minority prefer to find alternative accommodation throughout their time at university. Here are some of the advantages and disadvantages of 'living in':

Advantages
⇨ A small community means it is easy to meet people and make new friends.
⇨ You should be close to other university facilities and lecture halls.
⇨ You may feel safer and more secure living in halls.
⇨ Rooms will be regularly cleaned.
⇨ There is no need to provide your own furniture. Also, everything that is provided for you must meet a minimum quality standard.
⇨ If you are in catered halls, you will have all or some of your meals provided.

Disadvantages
⇨ Socialising and partying are part of student life for many people, but noisy neighbours and coursework deadlines are not a good combination!
⇨ It is easy to feel 'crowded', especially if you share a room. You may feel you have very little privacy or alone time.
⇨ Sharing bathroom and toilet facilities can sometimes be a trial if your roommate/neighbours are not the most hygienic of people!
⇨ If catered, meals will be served at a set time with little flexibility – you may find yourself missing meals if times are not convenient for you.

Shared accommodation

Most students will choose this option where halls of Residence are not available to them. It is very important to choose carefully when deciding who you will live with. Disputes between housemates are common and can make 'living out' an unpleasant experience. You should also be careful in choosing where you will live. Ask yourself the following questions:
⇨ Can I afford it? How will the monthly rent payments fit into my budget?
⇨ How far is it from places I need to get to regularly, such as lecture halls? If a lot of travelling will be involved, you should factor the cost of this into your budget too.
⇨ Is the landlord reasonable? Is he/she approved by the university? You should be asked to sign a contract, an agreement between you and the landlord. Check the terms of this carefully.
⇨ Will any bills be covered in my rental payments, e.g. gas, electricity, water? This is preferable to paying them separately. If these are not going to be covered in your rent, be sure to work out an agreement in advance with your housemates to make sure everyone is paying their share.
⇨ How much will the deposit be? Can I afford it? Could I afford to lose it?
⇨ Is the house in a decent state of repair?
⇨ Does it come fully or part furnished? If not, can I afford to rent or buy the furniture I need?
⇨ Have I factored expenses other than rent into my budget? Don't forget that unlike in halls, you will not have things like food or Internet access included in the amount you pay each month.

Renting as a lodger/host families

In some university towns, local people (called resident landlords or host families) will offer rooms in their own homes which can be rented by students. They will also provide meals. This is a popular option for some international students. Resident landlords must be approved by the university, and your institution's accommodation office should be able to match you to a suitable household on request or refer you to someone who can. This option has the following advantages and disadvantages:

Advantages
⇨ You will be accepted into a family home, which may help those who feel isolated from their own families upon going away to university.
⇨ The house and furnishings will be kept in good condition.
⇨ Furniture and white goods will be provided.
⇨ You should be able to get centrally-located accommodation at a reasonable rent.

Disadvantages
⇨ If you fall out with the owner or other members of the household, your stay could be very unpleasant.
⇨ You will not have the freedom you would have in shared accommodation or halls: for example, there may be restrictions on how much noise you can make, whether you can bring guests home and when you can use the household facilities (washing machine, bathroom etc).
⇨ You may feel cut off from campus life while living away from other students.

Note: for all accommodation enquiries, including what options are available to you and the costs involved, your first contact should be with your institution's accommodation office. Contact them as soon as you can after being accepted.
14 September 2009

© *Lisa Firth/Independence*

Government clamps down on shared accommodation

NUS and landlord outrage at government shared housing crackdown

Government proposals allowing councils to prevent people living in affordable shared houses have sparked furious opposition from landlords and students.

Ministers want to clamp down on houses of multiple occupation (HMOs) – homes rented by six or more unrelated people – as a part of a knee-jerk reaction to so-called 'studentification'. Problems with anti-social behaviour have arisen around high concentrations of HMOs, drawing complaints from locals about litter, noise and towns becoming empty during holidays.

> **Ministers want to clamp down on houses of multiple occupation (HMOs) – homes rented by six or more unrelated people – as a part of a knee-jerk reaction to so-called 'studentification'**

With a new consultation, the government is pressing ahead with measures to clear students out of residential areas. But immigrants, young professionals and others who rent HMOs will also be affected.

Property experts say that using planning laws to restrict HMOs will raise rents and drive out the students, young professionals and immigrants who rent them because they are affordable. Local businesses, particularly those which rely on student custom, also face being hit if students are driven out.

The move is also a wholesale contradiction of social integration policies, which the government have promoted to ensure that 'sink estates' are not recreated.

NUS has joined forces with property groups in condemning the plans as a 'nimby's charter' which would create student ghettos and dictate where people live based on their income.

The British Property Federation, National Landlords Association, Residential Landlords Association and NUS all say the proposals will not help and that similar moves failed in Northern Ireland.

The property industry wants a local management option to tackle the problems without further legislation. This could take into account local circumstances and offer a cost-effective solution to the problem.

Liz Peace, chief executive of the British Property Federation, said:

'You can't use the planning system for social engineering or to tackle anti-social behaviour. Only a tiny fraction of places suffer from a high concentrations of HMOs and using a broad brush approach to deal with different issues relating to anti-social behaviour makes no sense. It's vital that the property market is left flexible and we hope ministers will heed our warnings and reconsider going down the legislative route.'

Richard Price, director of operations, National Landlords Association, said:

'Planning is about buildings; homes are about people. Changing HMO planning regulations in order to allow small groups of vociferous local residents to discriminate against certain parts of the community is not helpful. Students, migrant workers and other people looking for affordable and more flexible accommodation are already a part of normal community life. Where there are problems, the current proposals would encourage local authorities to use a sledgehammer to crack a walnut.'

Wes Streeting, president of the National Union of Students said:

'Students live and work within their communities and contribute hugely to their local areas through charity work and campaigning on local issues, not to mention the massive boost they give to the local economy. These proposals would marginalise students by forcing them to pay private companies to live in large ghettos away from the rest of the community. This would do nothing to improve community cohesion.

'We must also remember that it is not just students who live in HMOs. Many young professionals and migrant workers share houses – it is extremely foolish to propose that we displace all of these people in the middle of a housing crisis. It is critical that the government takes a thoughtful and consultative approach to any problems that may have arisen in certain areas, rather than resorting to an ineffective headline-grabbing initiative.'

Alan Ward, chairman of the Residential Landlords Association, said:

'It's a classic case of nimbyism. Small but vociferous interest groups do not want students and migrants living near them. Their actions threaten the economic wealth of an area and the well-being of students, young people and the varied local businesses that depend on them. The move also threatens the mortgage value of rented properties. Planning permission can affect the marketability and value of property, forcing landlords to repay capital on their loans, or sell, resulting in loss of homes for tenants.'

Richard Chesterman, 23, a law graduate living in a shared house in Islington, north London, said:

'It's a disgrace that students could be face being barred from living in places just because they're students. There will always be a minority of people who cause trouble, but shipping everyone out of integrated society by banning the very shared houses that are affordable to young professionals would be massively damaging to everyone.'

The new rules on shared housing could make finding accommodation difficult for students

Chris Town, an HMO landlord in Leeds, said:

'HMOs are often large and therefore difficult and expensive to convert into a different use, such as flats or family housing. The government's proposal will put a severe constriction on the flexibility of property markets to adapt to local circumstances. As a result, it is possible that many derelict buildings will remain so as planning permission may be turned down on account of there being too many HMO properties in that area. The only result is likely to be decreased investment in local communities and increased blight.'

Amanda Williams, spokeswoman for UNITE, the UK's leading student accommodation developer, said:

'HMOs and purpose-built accommodation are both vital elements in the overall mix of private rented housing. However, there's a significant variation in quality standards and UNITE believes that all landlords should adhere to a professional management plan and a code of standards. Students must be provided with a choice of accommodation, and adequate and appropriate housing should be planned and targeted.'
9 August 2009

⇨ The above information is reprinted with kind permission from the British Property Federation. Visit www.bpf.org.uk for more information.
© *British Property Federation*

Squatting

Lifestyle choice or emergency housing? TheSite.org looks at the ins and outs of squatting

Squatting has been with us for many hundreds of years. The earliest cases can be traced back to 1381 when the Forcible Entry Act was passed. Following the end of the First and Second World Wars, some soldiers were forced to live in empty or derelict properties due to lack of decent housing.

Since the 1960s onwards squatting has been on the increase, with co-operatives and organisations springing up attracting people from all ages and backgrounds. In fact one of the better known squatting co-ops was a cluster of streets in the London Fields area of East London, which contained artists, the unemployed, students and even office workers living a nine-to-five lifestyle.

Why do squatters choose this particular way of life?

Sometimes it's because they have been made homeless and have been living on the streets or cannot face the local council's policy of housing the homeless in bed and breakfasts or hostels (that's if there is space). Others will also see it as a lifestyle choice.

According to the Empty Homes Agency there are roughly 784,000 empty homes in England.

The Advisory Service for Squatters offers legal and practical advice for anyone who may want to (or needs to) squat. They say: 'There is enough empty property other than homes, e.g. offices, to be converted into the equivalent of 700,000 homes. The number of squatters has been estimated recently to be as high as 30,000 (in the *Guardian*) but a more realistic estimate would be a little under 20,000, very few of whom are outside England and Wales, and most of those are in London.'

Hackney Council, which has had well-publicised battles with squatters in the past, had this to say on the subject: 'It's a fallacy that Hackney Council has lots of squatted premises anymore. These days we have very few. If we do we move very quickly to sort the problem out. We have a policy of regenerating empty properties.'

What you can and can't do:

⇨ Squatting is not strictly speaking a criminal offence, it is a civil offence against the landlord/owner of the property which to all intents and purposes means that it is an unlawful practice but not illegal.

⇨ You can be convicted of a criminal offence if you have caused damage to the property by gaining entry, covered under the Criminal Justice Act 1994.

⇨ The landlord/owners are well within their rights to evict squatters but they must go to a civil court in order to gain a possession order.

⇨ Squatters do have limited rights. A landlord cannot remove you by violent or forced means, only through the legal process.

⇨ Under squatters rights, if a property has been lived in for 12 years then it effectively becomes the property of the squatters.

The number one squatting rule, though, is to enter only empty and unused properties. Long gone are the days when holidaymakers would return home from a fortnight in the sun to find their homes had been taken over. These days it's more likely to be an empty and abandoned office block or warehouse.

⇨ The above information is reprinted with kind permission from TheSite. Visit www.thesite.org for more information.
© *TheSite*

Green Belt

Information from politics.co.uk

What is the Green Belt?

A Green Belt is an area of land protected from development. Green Belt land surrounds cities and towns to inhibit 'urban sprawl', prevent neighbouring towns merging into one another, preserve the countryside and the setting and character of historic towns, and assist in urban regeneration by promoting 'brownfield' development (development on derelict urban land).

Green Belt land is intended to be kept permanently open.

There are 14 designated Green Belts in England. To designate a Green Belt, a local authority must prove to the Office of the Deputy Prime Minister why normal planning and development control policies would not be adequate to protect a town from urban sprawl.

Green Belt land is protected both by normal planning controls and an additional presumption against 'inappropriate development' within its boundaries.

Background

The concept of the Green Belt was first mooted in 1935 by the Greater London Regional Planning Committee, which proposed providing 'a reserve supply of public open spaces and of recreational areas and to establish a Green Belt or girdle of open space'.

This was taken up by the Government in 1955 in Circular 42/55, which codified Green Belt provisions and extended the principle beyond London.

In 1988, Planning Policy Guidance 2 was issued, which reaffirmed the Government's commitment to the principle of the Green Belt, and added a requirement to take account of sustainable development. PPG2 was revised in 1995.

Controversies

Few contest the need to check urban sprawl, so the main controversy surrounding the Green Belt is the extent to which it is being eroded by planning decisions.

PPG2 leaves local authorities some leeway in interpreting what is 'inappropriate development' – there are exemptions for buildings used for agricultural and forestry, for 'essential' leisure facilities, for cemeteries, for 'limited' renovation of existing buildings and for 'limited' infilling of settlements within the Green Belt.

Countryside campaigners have long accused local authorities and the Government of allowing excessive development in Green Belts, and accuse them of undermining the principle.

In December 2006, the Government-commissioned Barker report said local authorities should consider allowing construction on Green Belt land.

The report, written by economist Kate Barker, said low-value agricultural land adjacent to towns and cities should not necessarily be classed as Green Belt. Building new houses in these areas would cut commuting time and be beneficial to the environment, the report said.

Statistics

⇨ 1,556,000 hectares of land make up England's Green Belt.
⇨ This is 12 per cent of the area of England.
⇨ The largest, surrounding London, comprises 486,000 hectares.
⇨ The smallest, surrounding Burton on Trent, consists of just 700 hectares.
⇨ Between 1997 and 2001, the Government considered 251 applications to develop Green Belt land.
⇨ It approved 119 of those applications.

(*Source: 1-4: PPG2 – ODPM, 1995; 5-6: The Independent, 2002*)

Quotes

'The Green Belt is a Labour achievement and we mean to build on it.'
John Prescott, Deputy Prime Minister (attributed)

'The Green Belt was meant to be an area where people could go for recreation and it has turned into a belt preventing and containing development.'
Professor Alan Evans, Bristol University (BBC Radio Four, 'Today', 4/12/01)

'There is national advice and statutory direction about what constitutes a departure from local plans, but it is essentially for local planning authorities to decide whether particular planning applications justify departure.'
Nick Raynsford, DTLR Minister (House of Commons, 22/4/98)

⇨ The above information is reprinted with kind permission from politics. co.uk. Visit www.politics.co.uk for more information.

© *politics.co.uk*

Greenfield development trends

Developers choosing to concrete over greenfield rather than brownfield sites

The countryside is being concreted over because the Government is making it too easy for developers to build on greenfield land rather than in urban areas, according to campaigners.

A University of Glasgow study of nine areas around the country found that where local authorities make greenfield sites available, developers choose that land over brownfield sites.

Councils are committed to building three million new homes by 2020

The Campaign to Protect Rural England (CPRE) said the study proved that developers are building on the countryside when urban areas need regeneration because the land is easier to build on and the houses can be sold for more.

By Louise Gray, Environment Correspondent

The group wants tighter restrictions on greenfield land and greater incentives for developers to build on brownfield land instead.

Kate Gordon, senior planner at the lobby group, said some local authorities are releasing greenfield land because of the pressure to meet targets.

Councils are committed to building three million new homes by 2020.

But she said brownfield land must be used first.

'We urge councils contemplating large-scale greenfield land releases not to proceed unless they are satisfied these will not harm prospects for redevelopment and regeneration.

'Tremendous potential still exists to make better use of brownfield opportunities and reap the long-term rewards in terms of urban renewal.

'Great care needs to be taken over the scale, location and timing of greenfield land release.'

The Department of Communities and Local Government said brownfield land remains the priority for development.

A spokesman said: 'The clear priority for development will remain previously-developed or brownfield land. The latest provisional estimates for 2008 show that 78 per cent of homes were built on brownfield land, up from 56 per cent in 1997. Targets are being exceeded but councils will need to continue to prioritise development away from greenfield sites.'

1 July 2009

© *Telegraph Media Group Limited (2009)*

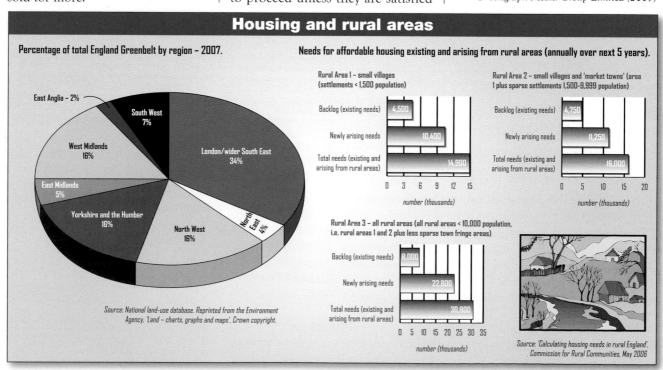

Housing and rural areas

Percentage of total England Greenbelt by region – 2007.

- East Anglia – 2%
- South West 7%
- West Midlands 16%
- London/wider South East 34%
- East Midlands 5%
- Yorkshire and the Humber 16%
- North East 4%
- North West 16%

Source: National land-use database. Reprinted from the Environment Agency, 'Land – charts, graphs and maps', Crown copyright.

Needs for affordable housing existing and arising from rural areas (annually over next 5 years).

Rural Area 1 – small villages (settlements < 1,500 population)
- Backlog (existing needs) 4,500
- Newly arising needs 10,400
- Total needs (existing and arising from rural areas) 14,900

number (thousands)

Rural Area 2 – small villages and 'market towns' (area 1 plus sparse settlements 1,500-9,999 population)
- Backlog (existing needs) 4,750
- Newly arising needs 11,250
- Total needs (existing and arising from rural areas) 16,000

number (thousands)

Rural Area 3 – all rural areas (all rural areas < 10,000 population, i.e. rural areas 1 and 2 plus less sparse town fringe areas)
- Backlog (existing needs) 8,000
- Newly arising needs 22,800
- Total needs (existing and arising from rural areas) 30,800

number (thousands)

Source: 'Calculating housing needs in rural England', Commission for Rural Communities, May 2006

What political parties say about housing policy

Forget the expenses row — how do the Conservatives, Liberal Democrats and Labour plan to solve the housing shortage?

The housing market is lower down on the political agenda than, say, the NHS or education, but issues such as the shortage of new homes, the inability of first-time buyers to get on the ladder and the length of social housing waiting lists are key vote winners — or losers. John Healey last week replaced Margaret Beckett as Housing Minister. Here is how the policies he has inherited stack up compared with the Opposition:

> **Issues such as the shortage of new homes, the inability of first-time buyers to get on the ladder and the length of social housing waiting lists are key vote winners**

New homes

The Government's target of three million new homes by 2020 remains unchanged; it has ring-fenced £400 million to restart stalled construction projects. But the Conservatives and the Liberal Democrats want to scrap centralised targets, with the former proposing financial incentives for local authorities who help to create new homes. The Liberal Democrats want to create community land trusts to make vacant public sector land available for 100,000 new affordable homes.

Garden-grabbing

The Government says that local authorities can already veto developments

By Francesca Steele

that they consider 'inappropriate' but recently launched a review to establish the level of the problem. The Tories and the Liberal Democrats want to redefine gardens as greenfield land to prevent them being developed.

Home information packs

The Government introduced home information packs (Hips) in 2007 with the aim of protecting buyers and preventing sales from collapsing. Since April, Hips must be available as soon as a property is marketed. The Government says that Hips are here to stay, despite criticism that they slow down sales by increasing the cost of offering your home for sale. Both

the Tories and Liberal Democrats want to scrap Hips but retain energy performance certificates, which are included in Hips.

Stamp duty

Alistair Darling has extended the 12-month stamp duty exemption on homes costing under £175,001 until December. Critics say that this is still too low a figure to help most first-time buyers (in London, the average property price is £302,411) but the Government says it has no plans to raise the threshold. The Tories want to scrap stamp duty on homes costing up to £250,000; the Liberal Democrats say that the system needs reform but do not yet have an alternative.

11 June 2009

© *Times Newspapers Ltd*

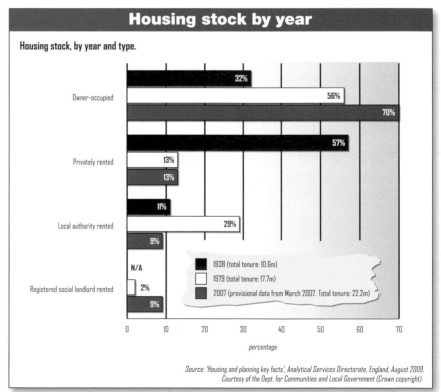

Housing stock by year

Housing stock, by year and type.

Owner-occupied — 32%, 56%, 70%
Privately rented — 57%, 13%, 13%
Local authority rented — 11%, 29%, 9%
Registered social landlord rented — N/A, 2%, 9%

- 1938 (total tenure: 10.6m)
- 1979 (total tenure: 17.7m)
- 2007 (provisional data from March 2007. Total tenure: 22.2m)

percentage (0, 10, 20, 30, 40, 50, 60, 70)

Source: 'Housing and planning key facts', Analytical Services Directorate, England, August 2009.
Courtesy of the Dept. for Communities and Local Government (Crown copyright).

Planning for buying a home

Buying a property will probably be your biggest single investment. So it's important to work out the total cost – not just the mortgage – and how much you can really afford. You also need to plan for increases in your future outgoings, like a rise in interest rates

'One-off' buying costs

Deposit

If you're a first-time buyer, most lenders insist on a deposit of five or ten per cent of the purchase price. Some will lend 100 per cent of the price, but they'll usually lend less and will charge a higher interest rate or 'higher lending charge'.

Surveyor's fees

You'll usually need to pay for the lender's basic valuation survey – the cost varies by lender and property value but is usually a few hundred pounds. To check the property's condition you'll need a more detailed survey for which you'll need to compare quotes.

Stamp Duty

If the purchase price is over £175,000 you pay Stamp Duty Land Tax of between one and four per cent of the property value. However, if the property is in a designated 'disadvantaged' area, you may not have to pay any Stamp Duty Land Tax at all. With some new builds the developer will pay your Stamp Duty Land Tax for you.

Solicitor's or conveyancer's fees

These cover searches and legal paperwork. Costs vary by area and/or the property value (or loan amount if it's remortgage) and include:

⇨ legal fees
⇨ land registry fees
⇨ local authority searches
⇨ drainage and environmental searches
⇨ administration costs.

Your solicitor will confirm the cost of the above fees.

Lender's arrangement fees

These vary by lender, but may include:

⇨ booking fee (limited offer mortgages only)
⇨ arrangement or completion fee (can often be added to the loan).

Lender's insurance premium

If you have a high percentage loan you may need to pay a one-off fee called a 'higher lending charge'. This protects the lender if you can't repay your mortgage. It's worked out as a percentage of what you borrow above the lender's higher lending charge limit, which is usually 80 or 90 per cent of the property value. The premium can be high; ask your lender or mortgage adviser. You can usually add it to the mortgage if it doesn't take you above the lender's maximum loan for the property value, but this will increase your interest charges.

Removals/moving in expenses

These vary according to:

⇨ where you live
⇨ the size of your property
⇨ how much furniture you've got
⇨ how far you're moving
⇨ how much packing you'll do yourself.

It's best to get several quotes, and always check that your remover is properly insured.

Ongoing monthly costs

Mortgage repayments

You'll need to budget for your monthly mortgage repayments – and take into account what effect a future change of interest rates would have on these.

If you have an 'interest only' mortgage, you'll usually also need to budget for monthly payments into an investment to pay off the loan at the end of the term.

Life insurance/mortgage protection cover

You might need to take out a life assurance policy such as 'term insurance' or a 'mortgage protection policy'. The monthly payments can be relatively low and the insurance pays off what you owe if you die before you've finished repaying the loan. Ask your mortgage

adviser for more details. (If you have a mortgage endowment policy, this includes life cover.)

You can also take out insurance that pays your monthly repayments if you're ill or out of work – but this can be expensive.

Buildings and contents insurance

Once you exchange contracts for your property you're responsible for insuring it. Your lender can insist that you have buildings insurance – but they can't make you buy their own. But in some cases, lenders can insist that you take out their insurance on completion.

Council Tax, utility and other regular bills

Don't forget that when you move, your monthly bills might go up.

Will you have enough to meet your new monthly outgoings?

You can use the Financial Services Authority (FSA) budget calculator on their website (www.fsa.gov.uk) to work out whether you'll have enough to meet your monthly payments. They also offer useful further tips on buying a home.

⇨ The above information is reprinted with kind permission from Directgov. Visit www.direct.gov.uk for more information.

© Crown copyright

Low-cost home-ownership options

Information from the Council of Mortgage Lenders

Not everyone can afford to buy a home on the open market. Recognising that most people want to become home-owners, the Government supports a number of schemes that provide people with a lower-cost way of buying a home. The main ones are set out below, and there is a much wider range of information and leaflets about low-cost home ownership available on the Department of Communities and Local Government website. If you are a 'key worker' you may also qualify for help to buy a home under special schemes.

> **Recognising that most people want to become home-owners, the Government supports a number of schemes that provide people with a lower-cost way of buying a home**

The 'right to buy'

If you rent your home from a social landlord such as a local authority or housing association, you may be able to buy your home from them. Some schemes offer discounts on the price of the property. The 'right to buy' is the most widely known scheme for buying your home from the council, and it offers discounts which can be quite large. Ask your landlord whether you qualify to buy your home.

Shared ownership

For some people, shared ownership is a suitable option to consider. Shared ownership is a 'half-way house' between buying and renting. You buy

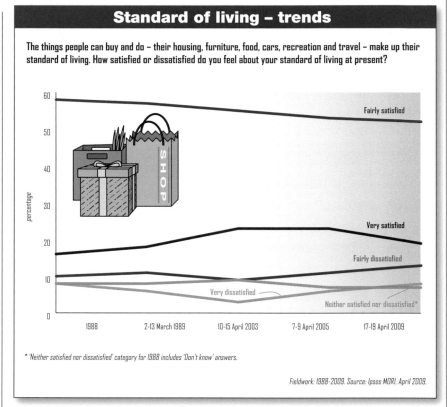

Standard of living – trends

The things people can buy and do – their housing, furniture, food, cars, recreation and travel – make up their standard of living. How satisfied or dissatisfied do you feel about your standard of living at present?

* 'Neither satisfied nor dissatisfied' category for 1988 includes 'Don't know' answers.

Fieldwork: 1988-2009. Source: Ipsos MORI, April 2009.

a chunk of the property – say 50% – with a normal mortgage from a lender. You then pay rent on the other chunk to a social landlord such as a housing association and you have the facility to buy another chunk at a later date – for example, when your earnings have risen thereby allowing you to qualify for a larger mortgage. There isn't always a big difference between the cost of shared ownership and the cost of full ownership, but it is definitely worth checking out this option if you would find it difficult to get a large enough mortgage to buy a home in the normal way. Shared ownership schemes are normally run through housing associations, who will have their own mechanisms for deciding who can qualify for them.

Homebuy

'Homebuy' is another form of part-ownership. Unlike shared ownership, on which the householder pays rent

on the proportion of the home they do not own, no rent is payable under Homebuy. Instead, you get a mortgage for 75% of the value of the property (sometimes 50% in Wales), but the remaining amount is held by a housing association, which reclaims its share when the property is eventually sold. This brings down the cost significantly, compared with full ownership. Like shared ownership, it gives you the opportunity to 'staircase' and buy extra chunks of the property, if and when you can afford to do this. But availability of Homebuy is very limited, although the Government hopes to expand the scheme significantly in the future.

⇨ The above information is reprinted with kind permission from the Council of Mortgage Lenders. Visit www.cml.org.uk for more information.

© *Council of Mortgage Lenders*

Young people and housing

Information from Citizens Advice

This information applies to England, Wales and Northern Ireland.

About this information

In this information child means someone aged under 14 and young person means someone aged 14 or over but under 18. Parent means someone with parental responsibility.

The law is not clear about whether someone who is under 18 can hold a tenancy and in practice, you may not be given a tenancy agreement if you're under 18

Council tax (England and Wales only)

If you are under the age of 18 you do not pay council tax.

Leaving home voluntarily

In most circumstances you can leave home without the consent of your parents or anyone with parental responsibility when you are 16. A parent or person with parental responsibility could go to court to try and force you to return home. However, it is unlikely that any court would order you to return home if you did not want to.

Being forced to leave home

If you are in conflict with your parents, you may feel you are forced to leave home. The legal position in this situation is complicated.

If you are under 16 and are forced to leave home, you can contact your local authority social services department. They will step in if they become aware of what is happening. The local authority may want to talk to your family to see what services it could provide to enable you to stay at home. If this is not possible, the local authority may try to find a relative to look after you or may offer to accommodate you. If you are at risk of suffering significant harm, the local authority may consider taking you into care.

Renting accommodation

The law is not clear about whether someone who is under 18 can hold a tenancy and in practice, you may not be given a tenancy agreement if you're under 18. As an alternative, you might be able to sign an agreement with a landlord for a licence. Holding a licence means that you have the landlord's personal permission, rather than a legal right, to stay in the accommodation.

Landlords, including housing associations and local authority housing departments, usually require a guarantor before giving a licence to someone under 18. If you move into local authority accommodation after leaving a children's home, the social services department will often be the guarantor.

If you move into rented accommodation, you may want to claim Housing Benefit. Although there is no age restriction on claiming Housing Benefit, the amount you can get if you are under 25 and have no children is restricted.

Buying accommodation

If you are under the age of 18, you will not be able to apply for a mortgage to buy accommodation. This is because you cannot own property in your own right although it may be held in trust for you until you come of age.

Homelessness

A local authority has a duty to provide accommodation to a young person who meets the criteria for being homeless.

A local authority also has a responsibility to look after you under The Children Act if:
⇨ no-one has parental responsibility for you; or
⇨ you are lost or abandoned; or
⇨ the person who has been caring for you is unable to continue

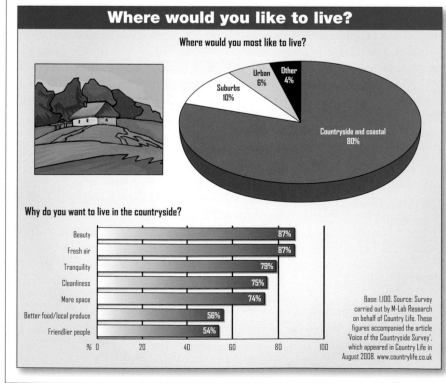

Where would you like to live?

Where would you most like to live?

- Other 4%
- Urban 6%
- Suburbs 10%
- Countryside and coastal 80%

Why do you want to live in the countryside?

- Beauty 87%
- Fresh air 87%
- Tranquility 79%
- Cleanliness 75%
- More space 74%
- Better food/local produce 56%
- Friendlier people 54%

% 0 20 40 60 80 100

Base: 1,100. Source: Survey carried out by M-Lab Research on behalf of Country Life. These figures accompanied the article 'Voice of the Countryside Survey', which appeared in Country Life in August 2008. www.countrylife.co.uk

to provide suitable care and accommodation; or

⇨ you are aged 16 or 17 and the local authority considers your welfare would be seriously threatened if it does not provide accommodation.

In most circumstances you can leave home without the consent of your parents or anyone with parental responsibility when you are 16

These rules also apply to asylum seekers.

If you don't understand English, the local authority must provide help and information in your own language.

If you are given accommodation in a children's home, the care you get must take into account your religious needs. For example, if you are Muslim, you should be offered Halal food.

Discrimination

It's against the law for someone who is providing you with accommodation or other housing services, for example housing advice, to discriminate against you because of your race, sex, disability, sexuality or religion.

Further help

Shelter (in England)
88 Old Street

London EC1V 9HU
Tel: 020 7505 2000
Freephone helpline: 0808 800 4444 (8am to midnight, seven days a week)
Fax: 020 7505 2169
Email: info@shelter.org.uk
Website: www.shelter.org.uk

Shelter Cymru (in Wales)
25 Walter Road
Swansea
SA1 5NN
Tel: 01792 469400
Freephone helpline: 0808 800 4444
(8am to midnight, seven days a week)
Fax: 01792 460050
Email: mail@sheltercymru.org.uk
Website: www.sheltercymru.org.uk
Shelter provides information and advice on housing issues.

Housing Rights Service (Northern Ireland)
Middleton Buildings
10-12 High Street
Belfast
BT1 2BA
Tel: 028 9024 5640
Fax: 028 9031 2200
Website: www.housingadviceNI.org
The Housing Rights Service website has pages specially aimed at young people between the ages of 16 and 25. These cover a range of housing problems. There is also a free email advice service for young people aged 16-25. You can access this through the website.

Who Cares Trust
Kemp House
152-160 City Road

London EC1V 2NP
Tel: 020 7251 3117 (admin)
Email: mailbox@thewhocarestrust.org.uk
Website: www.thewhocarestrust.org.uk
The Trust provides information and advice for young people in care or those who have recently left care.

Foyers
Foyers provide temporary hostel accommodation for young people, mostly aged 16-25, who are homeless or in housing need.

Foyer residents are also offered guidance, support, access to learning and help with finding work.

The average length of stay in a foyer is between nine and 12 months.

If you want to stay in a foyer, you can contact the nearest one to you and ask for an interview, or you can ask another agency such as your local housing authority, probation service or care home to refer you.

Some foyers will only accept young people who have been referred by their local housing authority.

To find details of your nearest foyer, contact:
The Foyer Federation
3rd Floor
5-9 Hatton Wall
London EC1N 8HX
Tel: 020 7430 2212
Website: www.foyer.net

⇨ The above information is reprinted with kind permission from Citizens Advice. Visit www.adviceguide.org.uk for up-to-date information on this and many other topics.

© Citizens Advice

Taking out a mortgage

I want to take out a mortgage to buy a house. What do I need to know?

This information applies to England, Wales and Northern Ireland.

If you're thinking about taking out a mortgage, there are several different options available. You should look into all the different options carefully to make sure you choose the right one for you. The most common types of mortgage are:

Repayment mortgage
This is a mortgage in which the capital borrowed is repaid gradually over the period of the loan. The capital is paid in monthly instalments together with an amount of interest. The amount of capital which is repaid gradually increases over the years while the amount of interest goes down.

Interest-only mortgage
With this type of mortgage, you pay interest on the loan in monthly instalments to the lender. Instead of repaying the loan each month, you pay into a long-term investment or savings plan which should grow enough to clear the loan at the end of the mortgage term and, in some circumstances, may even produce an additional lump sum. However, there is also a risk that it will not be worth enough to pay off the loan at the end of the mortgage term. This means you will have a shortfall and you will need to think about ways of making this up.

There are three main types of interest-only mortgages. These are:
⇨ an endowment mortgage;
⇨ a pension mortgage;
⇨ an ISA mortgage.

Islamic mortgage
With an Islamic mortgage, none of the monthly payments include interest. Instead, the lender makes a charge for lending you the capital to buy your property which can be recovered in one of a number of different ways, for example, by charging you rent.

Where to get a mortgage from
A mortgage could be available from a number of different sources. Some of the available options are:

⇨ building societies;
⇨ banks;
⇨ insurance companies. They only provide endowment mortgages (see above);
⇨ large building companies might arrange mortgages on their own new-build homes;
⇨ finance houses;
⇨ specialised mortgage companies.

For some groups of people, such as first-time buyers and key workers, it may also be possible to borrow some of the money you need to buy a home from other, government-backed sources. You will usually need to borrow the rest of the money from a normal mortgage lender such as a bank or building society.

Using a broker to get a mortgage
Instead of going directly to a lender such as a building society for a mortgage, a broker could be used. A broker may be an estate agent, or a mortgage or insurance broker. They will act as an agent to introduce people to a source of mortgage loan to help them buy a home.

You may want to use a broker if you find it difficult to get a mortgage directly from a lender.

There are rules about how much a broker can charge for their services.

If you're thinking about taking out a mortgage you should first make sure that you only borrow what can afford to pay back

---

Can you afford a mortgage?
If you're thinking about taking out a mortgage you should first make sure that you only borrow what you can afford to pay back. If you do not keep up the agreed repayments, the lender can take possession of the property.

⇨ Information from Citizens Advice. Visit www.adviceguide.org.uk for up-to-date information on this and many other topics.

© *Citizens Advice*

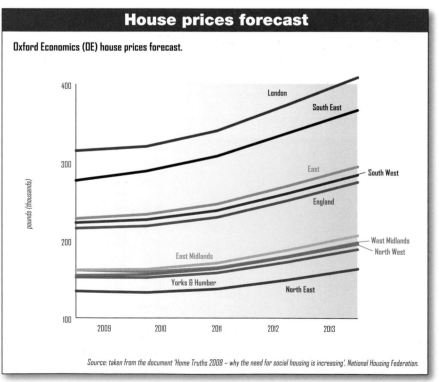

House prices forecast

Oxford Economics (OE) house prices forecast.

pounds (thousands) — 400, 300, 200, 100

London, South East, East, South West, England, West Midlands, North West, East Midlands, Yorks & Humber, North East

2009, 2010, 2011, 2012, 2013

Source: taken from the document 'Home Truths 2008 – why the need for social housing is increasing'. National Housing Federation.

Reform housing system to build 300,000 new homes

Information from the Local Government Association

More than 300,000 new homes could be built, providing a £72.5 billion boost to the economy over ten years, through root and branch reform of the housing finance system, a new report published today has revealed.

The Local Government Association, which represents more than 350 councils in England, will today (Tuesday 16 June) launch a major new housing campaign to give councils the freedom to build scores of new affordable homes and regenerate neighbourhoods across the country.

Demand for social housing is being fuelled by the recession. A survey of council leaders conducted by the LGA found that 57 per cent of authorities are seeing more people in need of social housing and 31 per cent expect to.

The LGA predicts that five million people could be on a social housing waiting list by 2011. In 2007, councils built less than 400 new houses. The Places You Want to Live campaign, which will be launched today at the Chartered Institute of Housing annual conference in Harrogate, calls for:

⇨ Councils to be able to retain rents and the proceeds of any council house sales;

⇨ Councils to have the financial independence to invest in their housing stock and stimulate the local economy;

⇨ Historic 'notional debt' – which councils are currently spending £1.3 billion a year servicing – to be cancelled;

⇨ Councils to have the same freedom as other social housing providers to borrow money to invest in new homes;

⇨ The government to stop setting tenants' rent and allow them to reflect local circumstances.

All the money councils collect in rent is currently transferred to central government coffers and either re-distributed to other parts of the country or spent on other projects. There is no guarantee the money is spent on housing. Analysis by the LGA has shown that if councils could retain this money they could, in just the current financial year, make 850,000 homes more energy efficient and save householders £160 on their energy bills.

Up to 90,000 additional affordable homes could be built by councils over the next five years if the system was reformed

Around £216 million of council tenant's rent will be retained by the Treasury in the current financial year – a figure that will rise to almost £1 billion by 2022/23. The LGA argues the building, repair and maintenance of council housing is being starved of cash. It wants the proceeds of tenants' rent to be retained locally and spent on improving housing for local people.

Up to 90,000 additional affordable homes could be built by councils over the next five years if the system was reformed. Over a ten-year period, the extra income from retaining tenants' rent would allow an extra 139,000 social houses to be built. If councils were also released from their historic debt and allowed to borrow against their assets this figure could rise to 309,000 – providing an enormous boost to the housing industry and the wider economy.

Cllr Margaret Eaton, Chairman of the Local Government Association, will tell the CIH conference today:

'Entire neighbourhoods could be transformed if councils were able to keep the rent they collect and the proceeds of council house sales. Thousands of homes could be built, improved or made more energy efficient if central government stopped taking this money.

'As the recession starts to bite and more and more people struggle to find a roof over the heads, it is more important than ever to give town halls more powers over housing. Councils want to create places where people are proud to live. Allowing councils to spend the rent they collect and the proceeds from council house sales would be a huge boost to the economy.

'The rent that the tenants pay to their council should be spent on their housing needs and those of local people. None of this money should be sitting in a Treasury vault. Councils with greater difficulties must not be left unsupported and may need additional funding, but this should not be at the expense of tenants in other parts of the country.

'Allowing councils to retain their rents would give tenants a real say over how their money is spent. It is ludicrous that someone living in Leicester could have their rent spent on housing in Leeds. Financial independence for local councils and local people will help create the places that people want to live in.'
16 June 2009

⇨ The above information is reprinted with kind permission from the Local Government Association. Visit www.lga.gov.uk for more information.
© *Local Government Association*

Community Self Build

Frequently asked questions

What is Community Self Build?

This is where a group of men and women in housing need join forces and become involved in the planning, design and building of their own homes.

What are the advantages of building your own home as part of a group?

As a group, provided that your members are in housing need, you are able to access funds via housing associations. The other advantages are:

⇨ Being involved in the planning, building and design of your homes;

⇨ Knowing in advance where you will be living – to plan for schools etc.;

⇨ Lower housing and running costs;

⇨ Living within a supportive community;

⇨ Having an opportunity to learn a range of skills.

For those without substantial savings and a job it is difficult to raise funds for the building of an individual home.

What is the ideal size for a Community Self Build group?

Ideally, keep your initial membership to no more than six people, because you cannot be certain what size of site/building will be available. Most groups should aim to build between six and 15 homes. Below six, there are too few homes over which to spread costs such as site supervision. Above 15, it becomes increasingly difficult for the group to keep together as a team.

How can our group meet up with other self builders and recruit new members?

The Community Self Build Agency organises visits to live self build projects, throughout the year. They are held in different locations and there is the chance to meet self builders, who are already working on site. Alternatively, we can put you in touch with a group who may be working on

a site nearer to you. The Agency has a database of those interested in self build who might want to join forces with you.

Why does my Local Authority ask me to form a self build group and then approach it again about self build?

Local Authorities need to know that there is a local demand for self build before considering whether to support the idea. Money for housing is tight and the Local Authority wants to be certain it is used wisely. Once you have a group of three or four people in similar circumstances, it should be possible to set up an initial meeting.

We have been told that to access money for site, work and fee costs, our group needs to form a partnership with a local registered housing association. How do we begin?

The best idea is to contact your Local Authority's Housing Association Liaison or Enabling Officer and ask for a list of housing associations, which have attracted funding regularly every year for homes in your area. Then contact the CSBA to see if any of these associations have shown an interest in Community Self Build. The Agency can help you broker a meeting. Prior to this, you need to have decided whether you are interested in a rented or shared ownership (part-rent/part-buy) projects. Outright ownership schemes are not funded via housing associations.

What are the key issues, which every self build group needs to consider?

Design, best use of time and skills, containing costs within budget and re-

lationships both within the group and with 'partner' organisations. All of these are interconnected and if addressed carefully at the beginning can be a recipe for a successful self build project.

What do other groups do about paying for meeting rooms and other expenses?

Your Town Hall may let you have a room at no charge or at a reduced cost. However, it is best to choose a meeting place, which is convenient for your members. Groups, even those with unemployed members, tend to start a kitty whereby everyone contributes a minimum of £5 per month. If you can show that some money has been raised from within, or by your group, it is so much easier then to ask for donations from elsewhere.

We're interested in refurbishing a building with other people. Are there such projects?

Yes, but there are fewer than new build. There have been some in Newcastle, Manchester, Leeds and East London.

How long does it take to build our own homes?

With good planning and supervision, this should only take between 12 and 15 months. However, the planning stage, including attracting funding, does take longer.

What causes the most delay for a self build group?

Finding a suitable site/building and complications on the transfer of ownership; this does not just apply to self build, but to a whole range of projects. With other projects, however, lives perhaps do not have to be put on hold until a start on site is achieved. If a housing association or a Local Authority is interested in promoting self build, it is important to identify a possible site as early as possible.

What should we do if our homes are taking longer to build than we expected?
You need to identify just why this is

the case and have a round-the-table discussion with your architect, quantity surveyor and housing association officer as soon as possible. Everyone involved needs to understand why this has happened and a decision made on how to address this. There is nothing as demoralising as being always 'behind' schedule.

Why is it that some housing associations are reluctant to become involved in self build?
Projects generally take more time and development staffs are already under pressure to spend all the money

allocated to their associations each year. Under-spends can affect future allocations of funding. However, it's more about how to pay for staff time. With the new allowance this should no longer be an issue. It also has to be recognised though, that any bad news on self build travels quickly whereas there's a lot of good news around.

⇨ The above information is reprinted with kind permission from the Community Self Build Agency. Visit www.communityselfbuildagency.org.uk for more information.
© *Community Self Build Agency*

Shared ownership

The cheapest way to own a home celebrates 30th birthday

Shared ownership schemes – the cheapest and most affordable way to own a home – are 30 years old today (Monday 27 July) after helping 155,000 households realise their dream of getting a foot on the property ladder.

The National Housing Federation has hailed the success of the scheme since the first home was sold under the ground-breaking initiative 30 years ago.

Thousands of low-to-middle in-come families have seized the chance to buy a share in a new home, since the scheme was launched on 27 July 1979, by Housing Minister John Stanley.

Shared ownership has helped key workers, first-time buyers and social tenants to live and work in areas which have seen house prices rocket well beyond what they could afford to pay on the open market, according to the National Housing Federation.

And now as the country is gripped by recession, housing associations – which build and manage the vast majority of shared ownership schemes – have found demand for shared ownership remains as high as ever.

Shared ownership is the most affordable and flexible form of low-cost home ownership on the market, with households buying a property earning an average of around £27,000 a year.

The scheme offers eligible people

the chance to buy between 25%-75% of a property from a housing association, and pay an affordable rent on the remaining share. People can increase the share they own over time and ultimately own the property outright.

Despite the current fall in house prices, the gap between house prices and the amount people can borrow continues to grow. Many people in permanent employment, earning a reasonable income, now find it impossible to get a mortgage.

Shared ownership has continued to offer an affordable option for thousands of people on moderate incomes during the recession.

But – despite strong demand – many lenders are refusing to lend to people wanting to buy shared ownership homes because they mistakenly view them as potentially 'sub prime'.

The Federation, which represents England's housing associations, estimates banks turned away up to £500m of valid business on shared ownership products last year – resulting in 9,000 low-cost homes being left empty, even though around 90,000 households had expressed an interest in moving into them.

The Federation has called on the Government to ensure state-owned and partially state-owned banks, such as Northern Rock, Lloyds TSB, RBS and Bradford and Bingley, take on a

social purpose and commit mortgage funds for people on low-to-moderate incomes who can afford to buy shared ownership homes.

Federation chief executive David Orr said: 'Shared ownership has been one of the country's great housing success stories and has helped 155,000 families onto the property ladder who would have had little or no chance to buy on the open market.

'30 years on and demand for shared ownership homes is as strong as ever, but the banks' current reluctance to lend on these properties means thousands remain empty and unsold.

'There's no evidence whatsoever that people buying shared ownership properties pose a greater risk of defaulting. This discrimination is denying thousands of people with good credit ratings the chance to own their own home.

'The banks which have been bailed out with billions of pounds of taxpayers' money should now take on a greater social role and take a lead in committing mortgage funds for shared ownership properties.'
27 July 2009

⇨ The above information is reprinted with kind permission from the National Housing Federation. Visit www.housing.org.uk for more.
© *National Housing Federation*

Self-help housing – making use of empty properties

Information from self-help-housing.org

'Self-Help Housing' involves people negotiating with the owners of empty properties to bring them back into use on a short term basis, until they're needed. This could be for a period of months or even years, depending on what is planned. It differs from 'Community Self Build' where permanent homes are constructed from scratch.

Where do properties come from?

It depends on what's empty in your locality, but they could be:
- Properties owned by a local authority or housing association that are awaiting improvement or redevelopment.
- Properties owned by other public bodies which are redundant or may have been bought up in advance of delayed capital project, such as a new road scheme, hospital or school.
- Properties in private ownership that are standing empty.

You may be able to identify a property or properties for yourself, or you may want to approach one of the owners above and ask them what might be available.

How long might they be available and will the owner charge rent?

The 'life' of the property will depend on what is ultimately going to happen to it, but it could be anything from a matter or months to five, ten or even 15 years. It's likely not to be practical to take on anything with too short a life (perhaps less than a year) and it may be that it's offered initially for a certain period, which can be extended as time goes by.

The owner will usually charge some rent but the amount usually depends on:
- who owns the properties;
- why they are empty; and
- what condition they are in.

Either way, the rent needs to be small enough to make it economically viable to take them over and carry out any repairs that need doing.

Setting up a self-help project and putting forward a proposal

To persuade the owner to let you take on the property, you'll most probably have to set up some sort of project, since they usually won't hand over properties to an individual or even several individuals. They usually prefer to enter into an agreement with an 'organisation' of some sort, which has clear aims and objectives (e.g. to house and support certain sorts of people).

In addition, you may need to put forward a proposal in writing, setting out how you intend to use and run the properties. This will deal with issues such as:
- how you propose to repair and manage the property;
- the benefits to the owner and community in terms of bringing the property back into use; and
- your willingness to hand back the property at the end of the agreement.

What about funding for any necessary repairs?

How much money will be needed to bring a property back into use will obviously depend on the state of the property and for how long it's available.

Many projects finance repairs by simply 'recycling' the money that will be received from renting them out over the life of the property, and using it to pay for whatever works are necessary. However, depending on the circumstances it may be possible to get a grant from a local authority or via a housing association to carry out the works.

It may also be possible to get grants from local charities to cover some or all of the costs.

How can repairs be organised?

Depending on the extent of any repairs that need to be carried out and the amount of money available, it's possible to either use builders, do the work yourselves or to opt for some sort of combination of the two.

To get the electrics, gas and roofing done a builder will usually be necessary, but there are lots of repairs that can be undertaken by prospective occupants, subject to the necessary health and safety considerations.

Who can be housed?

Once you've negotiated the use of the properties, then the decision will largely be yours, subject to any conditions that the landlord may specify.

By and large, those interested in self-help housing are people, who for one reason or another, are not going to be offered a permanent tenancy with a local authority or housing association. These are likely to be single people who are not deemed to be 'vulnerable', couples, people leaving institutions of one kind or another, refugees, etc.

Because of the short-term nature of the accommodation, it's usually best to avoid housing people who are in some way vulnerable or have dependents which mean they that need long-term accommodation.

- The above information is reprinted with kind permission from self-help-housing.org. Visit http://self-help-housing.org for more information.

© self-help-housing.org

Gen Y wants freedom from flat ownership

'Conti-rental' trend for more flexible accommodation

18 to 30-year-olds are a generation of renters compared to their older counterparts, according to new research by the Association of Residential Letting Agents (ARLA).

Young females were keener to get on the property ladder, with 45.2% having bought before they turned 25, whilst only 32% of men could claim the same

---

A survey of over 1,800 people revealed that double the amount of the younger generation – approximately a third (30.8%) – have rented three or four properties, whilst only 17.5% of Generation X had rented a similar number at the same age. 34.2% of Gen Y-ers that currently live in rented accommodation confessed that they enjoy independence from property ties.

A further 31.6% enjoyed the flexibility to move around. However, only 8% thought it wasn't important to eventually own their own property. There were more men who had never paid rent for a property – 32.3% had opted to stay in the family home – whilst 75% of females were making their own way in the world and had either bought or were in rented accommodation.

Young females were keener to get on the property ladder, with 45.2% having bought before they turned 25, whilst only 32% of men could claim the same. 21% of 18-to-30s stated that they wanted to continue renting for the foreseeable future.

Ian Potter, Operations Manager of ARLA, said: 'The research reveals a generation that want to be upwardly mobile and free from ties. Attitudes towards renting have changed in the UK and perhaps we're becoming more like our fellow Europeans, who tend to rent rather than buy.

'This trend of being "conti-rental" recognises that renting should no longer be perceived as a waste of money, but simply as an alternative lifestyle choice to being tied to property for the long term. Today's graduates, more than ever, are looking for work that involves travel and opportunities to move around, renting allows them to operate more freely in a flexible job market.'
31 July 2009

⇨ The above information is reprinted with kind permission from the Association of Residential Letting Agents (ARLA). Visit www.arla.co.uk for more information.
© *Association of Residential Letting Agents (ARLA)*

Housing poverty

Council tenants who look for work should be given stake in their homes – new report

Up to ten million social housing tenants should be rewarded for decent behaviour by giving them a stake in their property under radical new plans designed to break down the 'ghettos' of Britain's council estates, according to a new report from the think-tank set up by the former Conservative leader Iain Duncan Smith.

The 134-page report charts how many of the stable and prosperous working class communities of the 1960s and 1970s have degenerated into sink estates trapping their tenants into lives on benefits from which few ever escape.

It proposes incentives designed to reduce welfare dependency and enable the poorest families to begin to acquire assets and join the mainstream of society.

'Over the years, our housing system has ghettoised poverty'

Housing policy should be used as an active lever in moving people from welfare to work, rebuilding mobility and ending the financial apartheid created by a benefits system that penalises savings.

'Housing policy must be seen as part of broader social policy which aims to get people back to work and in a position to help themselves, their families and communities... Currently, social housing can act as a huge disincentive to going back to work, and is blocking mobility,' Mr Duncan Smith says in a preface to the report from the Centre for Social Justice.

'Over the years, our housing system has ghettoised poverty, creating broken estates where worklessness, dependency, family breakdown and

addiction are endemic,' Mr Duncan Smith adds.

The report cites polling conducted by YouGov for the CSJ that shows that 70 per cent of those who pay their social housing rent on time want to own their own home.

Yet the benefits system denies realisation of this aspiration, which would have a wider beneficial impact on run-down, crime-ridden estates.

The report proposes that sitting tenants who pay their own rent and make a contribution to society should be given discounts on the purchase price of their property to help them buy it outright or in part.

But it goes further by calling for economic analysis of the proposal that tenants who make a genuine effort to get off benefits and find work should be rewarded by the carrot of an increasingly large equity stake in their home.

The reports says: 'We encourage an incoming government to look at releasing some of the value in social housing to sitting tenants who pay their own rent and make a contribution to the community. This could take the form of a discount on the purchase price for those moving to outright or shared ownership.'

'However, the most radical approach is also the most important. We recommend that economic analysis be commissioned into the rewarding of constructive behaviour in the community, including, but not limited to, a genuine effort on the part of a social housing tenant to find work, by giving social housing tenants

increasingly larger equity stakes in the home.'

The report adds: 'Helping to lift the most vulnerable out of income poverty is by no means easy, but it is certainly easy relative to helping them escape asset poverty.

'Yet the potential benefits from helping the most vulnerable escape are immense. The ownership of an asset encourages a series of behavioural changes. Those who own are more likely to protect their assets, to protect their position of ownership and to engage in constructive behaviours that enable their assets to be protected and enlarged: behaviours that benefit themselves, their families and the community at large.

'We need to find a way to end the cycle of destructive behaviour on our social housing estates. This must involve fostering a real link between aspiration and behavioural shift. Finding a way to relieve asset poverty... is tantamount to offering hope. Along with this hope comes the incentive to behave more constructively, to take action and responsibility for one's own life. Society will benefit in every way from these behavioural changes...

'Having a stake in a home is both a privilege and a responsibility. It would inculcate the values of constructive social behaviour and create, from the vicious cycle, a virtuous cycle that encourages social housing tenants to improve their family's future.

'While occupied by social tenants social housing has very little value. Turning tenants into owners releases

the value of the home and allows the most vulnerable in our society to benefit.'

The report also makes a series of other recommendations aimed at broadening the social mix of housing estates, relieving inequality and meeting the aspirations of a majority of low-income social housing tenants to own their own homes through, for instance, wider access to shared ownership schemes.

In a foreword to the report, Kate Davies, chairman of the group of experts who have produced *Housing Poverty – From Social Breakdown to Social Mobility*, calls for an end to Whitehall targets for building new social homes and advocates a 'localised revolution in housing supply'.

The report says: 'Councils need to be free to decide how housing resources are deployed in their areas, balancing the needs to improve existing council homes, build new ones and work with the private and not-for-profit sectors to provide a range of lower cost housing options for local residents.'

As part of this shift in power from the centre to local authorities, the law should be changed to end the 'stifling requirement' that social housing tenancy be secure for life. Instead, councils and housing associations should be allowed the flexibility to adapt tenure agreements to meet the needs and aspirations of clients.

Mrs Davies adds in her foreword: 'Social housing has come to reinforce inequality and social division in society; the poor more than ever have become ghettoised in social housing estates, getting relatively poorer while the better off acquire an appreciating asset and can pass their housing wealth down to the next generation.'

The report charts the way social housing has become the preserve of the poor and vulnerable over the last 30 years as a result of deliberate Government policy of insisting that councils and housing associations allocate properties to those in greatest need.

The number of homes rented from councils and housing associations peaked at 5.5 million in 1979 and has fallen steadily since then to 3.9 million in 2007, providing accommodation for an estimated 9.8 million people. Some 1.6 million households were on waiting lists last year.

In the early 1980s, council tenants' average income was 73 per cent of the national average. Today two thirds of social housing tenants are among the poorest 40 per cent of the population. Between 1981 and 2006, the proportion of social housing tenants of working age in full-time employment fell from 67 per cent to 34 per cent, the report says. Two thirds of social housing tenants receive housing benefit even though their rents are about one half of the private sector.

Meanwhile, children growing up on housing estates are enmeshed in a culture of worklessness. More than half of the heads of households aged 25-54 are not doing any paid work and a quarter are classed as permanently sick or disabled. Nearly one in five social housing tenants are lone parents. More than four fifths of social housing tenants are still there ten years later.

The housing crisis has been compounded by other factors – growth in population and household formation and sharply rising house prices – only now being checked by the recession. On the official index, housing has become twice as unaffordable over the last decade.

Home ownership has stalled and is declining rapidly among the young. The proportion of owner-occupiers among the 20-24 age range fell from 41 per cent in 1984 to 20 per cent in 2004.

Three key propositions underpin the report: social housing is not a 'desirable destination'; private ownership of property is preferable to state ownership; and councils should be freed from central control and targets and allowed to develop housing policies meeting local needs.

Mrs Davies says that social housing should be 'a dynamic resource, playing a part in helping people get back on their feet and on with their lives'.

'From homelessness, they would take a temporary house, before renting, moving on when possible to shared equity or outright ownership.

'We believe that this should be the normal path to self-sufficiency for the vast majority. Help with housing costs is necessary, but a permanent social tenancy is not.'

Polling for the report by YouGov found that many social housing tenants expressed dissatisfaction with their neighbourhood.

Over 20 per cent of social housing tenants on estates where flats are the norm said that drug dealers and users were a problem. Such people were far more fearful of crime and burglary than the general population and nearly a half did not trust their neighbours.

2 December 2008

⇨ The above information is reprinted with kind permission from the Centre for Social Justice. Visit www.centreforsocialjustice.org.uk for more information on this and other related topics.

© *Centre for Social Justice*

Give council tenants the right to move

Information from Policy Exchange

By Tim Leunig

Council and housing association tenants get little choice over where they live and are rarely able to move: many are in properties that do not suit their individual needs and preferences.

This can and should change. In *The Right to Move*, a paper published today, Policy Exchange argues that social tenants should have the right to move, the right to require their landlord to sell their current home and use the money to buy a place chosen by the tenant.

The new property would be owned by the landlord, and rented out as before. Tenants would be better off: they would get to live in a house of their choice.

The value of the landlord's portfolio does not change – only its location. Of course, if a Lambeth tenant moves to Croydon, Lambeth will need to subcontract the maintenance to Croydon, but this is hardly difficult. Landlords could veto properties with disproportionately expensive maintenance – thatched cottages and the like. When the tenant leaves social housing, Lambeth could sell the Croydon property and buy one in Lambeth as necessary.

There are important advantages for society.

First, all tenants would gain a real stake in their house and area. Since they might one day want to move, they have an incentive to look after both, to report little problems before they become big ones, and an incentive to stand up against anti-social behaviour that plagues too many social housing estates.

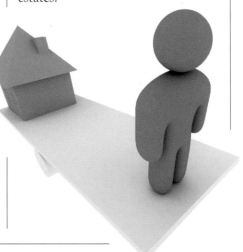

Second, when social tenants move out of estates they would integrate with those living in other tenures. In addition, as some estate properties are sold on the open market, those estates would become more mixed, leading to better-integrated communities.

Third, social tenants could, for the first time, move easily for job-related reasons, both within their own town and further away. This is good for them, but it is also good for society more generally, since it raises tax revenues and cuts benefit spending.

Fourth, poorer families could do what many middle-class families do when they have children: move to areas with more space and better schools. Flats in city centres are generally as valuable as houses in the suburbs, allowing many families to move.

Council and housing association tenants get little choice over where they live

The only question is who should pay the costs of moving: selling fees, valuations and legal costs. Given bulk buying, these amount to around £1,000. The gains to society from greater social integration, as well as higher levels of employment, make a case for these to be subsidised to encourage social tenants to move, and we suggest that the state should allow tenants a 'free move' once every five years. Those who wish to move more often would have to pay the fees themselves.

The right to move is about freedom, dignity and opportunity. It is about giving the same choices to those who are poor as to those who are middle class. It has the potential to transform the lives of millions of people living in social housing, by allowing them to decide where they live.
30 January 2009

⇨ The above information is reprinted with kind permission from Policy Exchange. Visit www.policyexchange.org.uk for more information.
© *Policy Exchange*

Eco-towns glossary

Definitions for some of the most common terms used in discussions about eco-towns

'Affordable housing'
The term 'affordable housing' can cover a number of different types of housing provision, including below market-rate housing both for rent and for purchase, housing provided for rent by registered social landlords (RSLs) and 'shared ownership' schemes whereby residents pay for a proportion of the property, in order to gain a foothold on the housing market, and can then increase the proportion of the property they hold in order to allow a larger deposit to be accumulated.

'Zero-carbon' towns
Eco-towns aim to be examples of best practice developments. As such they must adhere to strict criteria, one of the most important being steps to combat climate change. Each eco-town will be required to be 'zero-carbon' over the course of a year and this means that over the course of a year the net carbon emissions from all energy use from buildings in the development are zero.

'Brownfield' and 'greenfield'
The term 'brownfield' refers to a previously developed piece of land (including the entire footprint from buildings and associated infrastructure) – for example land previously used for industrial purposes – these sites are often, but not always, in pre-existing towns and urban areas. The term 'greenfield' refers to land which has not previously been built on, for example land currently being used for agriculture or left to nature – these sites are often in the countryside.

'Greenbelt'
The meaning of 'greenbelt' is distinct from 'greenfield' – it is a designation for land surrounding certain large cities and built-up areas, designated as such with the aim of keeping the space open or mostly undeveloped.

'Green infrastructure'
A network of green space, new and existing greenery both urban and rural, supporting natural processes and providing a pleasant green living environment for everyone. Examples include street trees and grass verges, as well as hedgerows and flowerbeds.

⇨ The above information is reprinted with kind permission from Directgov/Department for Communities and Local Government. Visit http://ecotownsyoursay.direct.gov.uk for more information.
© *Crown copyright*

An introduction to eco-towns

Information from Directgov

Eco-towns are proposed new communities to provide between 5,000 and 15,000 new homes. As well as being affordable, well-designed, well-built and 'green', they will be well linked to existing towns and have facilities such as schools, health centres, parks and allotments.

Why eco-towns?

The advantages of eco-towns are:
- they will help relieve the need for new housing;
- at least 30 per cent of housing will be affordable;
- the housing will be of a high quality;
- they are designed to be environmentally friendly to tackle climate change, as well as being attractive communities to live in.

How are eco-towns 'green'?

Everyday actions – like heating your home or driving your car – consume energy and produce greenhouse gas emissions, such as carbon dioxide, which contribute to climate change. Strict environmental building standards and low carbon energy sources will be used to make sure that eco-towns have the minimum impact on the environment.

Setting standards

Rigorous standards are being proposed to make sure eco-towns are greener developments.

These are the toughest environmental standards ever set for new developments in the UK:
- homes and buildings will be specially designed and built so that they need less energy to run – making them cheaper for residents, as well as more environmentally friendly;
- net carbon dioxide emissions across all the buildings within an eco-town, measured over a year, should be zero or less than zero (because the carbon dioxide emissions will be offset by local green energy production using energy sources like wind or solar power).

Using low-energy sources

Eco-towns will use a range of low and zero carbon energy sources:
- natural sources within the town such as wind and solar energy;
- methods which use energy which could otherwise be wasted such as combined heat and power plants.

The UK has a strong tradition of creating new towns and cities when the population grows and people need more homes

As well as lowering energy consumption, eco-towns should also use measures to:
- minimise water use;
- reduce waste.

Living 'green'

Eco-towns will be planned so the local community lives in a greener environment. There will be lots of green space where children can play and residents can take a walk and enjoy the open air (in fact, 40 per cent of every eco-town must be green space – at least half of which must be open to the public).

In addition:
- each eco-town will have schools, shops, businesses and community facilities that you can walk to – or are just a short ride away by public transport;
- there will be a variety of transport and travel options to promote alternatives to car journeys;
- a minimum of one job per household should be available which can be reached using public transport, by bicycle or on foot.

The history of new communities

The UK has a strong tradition of creating new towns and cities when the population grows and people need more homes. In response, architects, town planners and engineers have built new communities, from the great public buildings in Victorian times, through to the new towns in the post-war era, like Welwyn Garden City and Milton Keynes.

There are already some eco-developments in England. Poundbury, a development to the west of Dorchester in Dorset, has been designed for eco-living and features eco-homes. Other eco-developments include Upton in Northampton and the zero-carbon BedZED community in Surrey.

Eco-towns around the world

Successful eco-towns are being created across the world to help tackle global warming. There are already similar developments in Sweden and Germany. Other countries are working on developments which follow strict environmental standards.

Eco-towns will make the UK part of a global effort to produce affordable, environmentally friendly homes. Your input in the consultation process can help shape the nature of these new communities – to provide the homes needed by the next generation in the most environmentally sensitive way possible.

- The above information is reprinted with kind permission from Directgov. Visit www.direct.gov.uk for more information.

© Crown copyright

Eco-towns approved amid country devastation fears

The locations for four proposed eco-towns have been confirmed amid claims they will 'devastate the countryside', increase traffic congestion, impinge on wildlife habitats and exacerbate flooding

Four developments of more than 5,000 homes each are proposed for a former RAF base near Norwich in Norfolk; at an old army barracks in East Hampshire; on the outskirts of Bicester in Oxfordshire; and on the site of an old china clay mine near St Austell in Cornwall.

The Prime Minister hailed the 'revolutionary' developments but the Government's own documents detail continuing concerns over whether the sites are 'green' enough, with the potential that they may actually damage the environment in building new roads and access to water sources.

Campaigners, backed by celebrities like Tim Henman's father Tony and Judi Dench, said they were relieved that only four sites were going ahead but remained concerned about the millions of pounds spent developing a scheme for as few as 20,000 homes.

The new towns will now have to go through the planning process. If they are successful it will result in the first Government-backed green new towns in the world. The developments will be made up of 40 per cent green space like parks and less than 50 per cent of travel will be by car. Wind turbines and woodchip boilers will power homes. Residents will heat water for showers with solar panels and reuse the water for plants, collect food scraps for burning to generate electricity and use sewage to heat homes.

A further two towns in Rossington in South Yorkshire and North-East Elsenham in Essex also have Government support in developing bids for eco-town status.

Gordon Brown said the 'revolutionary' eco-towns will transform how people live. Eco-towns will be made up of 30 per cent affordable

By Louise Gray, Environment Correspondent

housing. Schoolchildren will not have to walk more than 800 metres to the nearest 'zero carbon school', commuters will be alerted to when the next bus is arriving via an electronic indicator in the home and cycle paths will make it easier to bike to work.

The four eco-towns could be built by 2016 with a further six in place by 2020

'Eco-towns will help to relieve the shortage of affordable homes to rent and buy and to minimise the effects of climate change on a major scale,' he said. 'They will provide modern homes with lower energy bills, energy efficient offices and brand new schools, community centres and services.'

Is the English countryside under threat from eco-towns?

The four eco-towns could be built by 2016 with a further six in place by 2020.

However, there are already problems with each of the four sites. North-west Bicester is in an area susceptible to flooding and there are issues around dealing with more sewage in the system, Rackheath in Norfolk has raised concerns about more congestion around Norwich, the China Clay Community in St Austell will need transport links and Whitehill Borden in East Hampshire could impact on important areas for wildlife nearby.

Kate Gordon, senior planner at the Campaign to Protect Rural England, said: 'They will have a devastating impact on the countryside if they are built in the wrong place. Eco-towns are major developments that require infrastructure. They should not generally be built on greenfield sites.'

Grant Shapps, the Tory shadow housing minister, also described the eco-towns scheme as a 'complete farce' because the houses in the new settlements would not have to be as green as all other new properties built after 2016.

Mr Shapps said: 'Buried away in the statement is a line that says these homes can be built to a lower level of greenness and sustainability than all other homes built at the same time that these eco-towns will come online.'

He said that while all homes from 2016 will have to be built to the Government's zero-carbon level of six, the eco-town houses constructed before that date will only have to meet the lower level of four.

Mr Shapps added: 'So, these eco-towns are less eco-friendly than all other homes that will be built at the same time.'

John Healey, the housing minister, acknowledged the point but said the eco-town houses would be more green than most newbuild homes at present.

He added that the environmental friendliness of the houses only formed part of the broader range of benefits offered by the eco-towns.

A spokesman for the Department of Communities and Local Government (DCLG) said: 'Eco-towns will also have to achieve zero-carbon status across the entire development, which includes shops, offices and schools as well as housing.'

Four developments of more than 5,000 homes each are proposed

It cost the DCLG £3 million to bring together the case for eco-towns. The four sites that have been given the go-ahead have access to £60 million as well as further funds to build schools and public infrastructure. The rest of the money needed to build the houses will come from developers.

Stephen Joseph, executive director of the pressure group Campaign for Better Transport, said: 'Whether these eco-towns will be sustainable is down to the detail on transport provision.

'If built around major new roads – as the local council wants the Rackheath scheme to be – and without good public transport, local services, car-free areas and convenient cycling routes at their heart, these schemes will not deserve the eco-towns brand.

'It should be possible for people to live in these places without having to own a car.'

Friends of the Earth executive director Andy Atkins said: 'Government is starting to put the "eco" back into eco-towns – plans now include plenty of open space and access to decent public transport.

'But the bigger challenge is to ensure that all new housing is built to the highest environmental standards.'

17 July 2009

© Telegraph Media Group Limited (2009)

Getting real about sustainable housing

By Ben Ross, Senior Sustainability Advisor, Forum for the Future

forum for the future
action for a sustainable world

With the 26 million homes in the UK generating around 27% of the nation's carbon emissions, and being considered one of the easier areas for reduction, there's clearly a lot of work to be done. The main focus over the last few years has been on improving the performance of new buildings, through tightening building regulations and the new code for sustainable homes. While the target (and definitions) of all new-build homes being zero carbon by 2016 is clearly challenging, it gives us a mark to aim for.

But research by BRE has suggested that over 40% of new build do not achieve current building regulations, and even initial good performance rapidly decreases (Good Homes Alliance). So it's not only design that needs to evolve significantly, but also materials, component manufacture and approaches to on-site construction. Demands on the market like this should drive innovation and the rapid development of new skills and supply chains.

While this is a critical part of national carbon reduction strategy, the elephant in the room is the poor performance of our existing housing stock. But it seems that the majority of people are standing with their backs to it and are trying hard not to notice it's sheer size...this isn't any old elephant, it's a fully grown woolly mammoth. But recognition is certainly growing with just this week the Communities and Local Government Select Committee launching the 'Existing Housing and Climate Change report' calling on Ministers to 'engage fully' with our existing stock and stating, 'The Government must not be complacent.' There have been a number of programmes to improve the energy efficiency of our homes but, when you factor in the increasing expectations we have, in terms of the temperatures of our homes and the growth in consumer goods, we're pretty much standing still!

The majority of the UK's homes fall into Energy Performance Certificate bands of E, F or G, with an average SAP (the Government's Standard Assessment Procedure for energy rating of dwellings) rating in the high 40s. Recent research by Forum for the Future and URBED recommends an annual refurbishment rate of at least 1% (260,000 homes each year) by 2011, rising to at least 3.5% (910,000) by 2016. This level of activity would need to be maintained for a minimum of 20 years, in order to raise all domestic property into band C, with a SAP rating of at least 70. This is the magnitude of change that is required to give the UK a chance of meeting national carbon reduction targets.

To be effective in targeting the 70% of homes that are owner occupied it is vital that improving energy efficiency is both easy and convenient, and that all opportunities and points of influence, such as major refurbishment works, are taken. Providing a clear, structured and consistent approach will present huge opportunities for all, from community-based social enterprises to the wider business community.

7 April 2008

⇨ The above information is reprinted with kind permission from Forum for the Future. Visit www.forumforthefuture.org for more information.

© Forum for the Future

⇨ The average age of first-time buyers who do not receive financial backing from relatives has risen sharply from 33 to 37 in the past two years. (page 1)

⇨ The Government has set a housing target of 240,000 homes per year by 2016, and a total of three million homes by 2020. (page 2)

⇨ Residents in some areas of rural England would have to wait 280 years to be allocated a new home because so few new properties are being built, a study reveals. (page 3)

⇨ Nearly a third of men and a fifth of women aged 20 to 34 live with their parents, the Office for National Statistics reports. (page 4)

⇨ Almost seven in ten first-time buyers in the UK have given up hope of ever owning their own home, according to new research published by PropertyLive.co.uk. (page 5)

⇨ The government is certain to break its long-standing promise to be building 70,000 affordable homes a year by 2010-11, according to the *Guardian*. (page 6)

⇨ In June 2009, leading economist Ian Shepherdson predicted repossessions will jump to between 100,000 and 120,000 per year by 2011, as levels of unemployment increase and people's incomes become squeezed. (page 7)

⇨ Around 6.5m people – or one in ten of the population – will be on social housing waiting lists in England by 2020 unless urgent action is taken, according to new figures. (page 8)

⇨ Four generations ago, families in social housing included almost the full social range. Council and housing association homes offered high quality. However, from the 1960s, home ownership took over from social housing as the main type of housing for families. (page 9)

⇨ Less than two per cent of the occupants of council houses or housing association homes arrived in Britain in the past five years. New immigrants are far more likely to be found in privately-rented accommodation. (page 12)

⇨ Nearly a third of households with children in England live in poor housing. (page 13)

⇨ Over one million children are now trapped in overcrowded housing, a rise of 54,000 in the last two years, Shelter has revealed. (page 14)

⇨ New homes are failing to provide enough space for everyday activities. (page 15)

⇨ 94 per cent of lettings agent respondents to the ARLA Members' Survey of the Private Rented Sector reported an increase of property coming onto the rental market because it could not be sold. (page 17)

⇨ Ministers want to clamp down on houses of multiple occupation (HMOs) – homes rented by six or more unrelated people – as a part of a knee-jerk reaction to so-called 'studentification'. (page 19)

⇨ Squatting has been with us for many hundreds of years. The earliest cases can be traced back to 1381 when the Forcible Entry Act was passed. Following the end of the First and Second World Wars, some soldiers were forced to live in empty or derelict properties due to lack of decent housing. (page 20)

⇨ 1,556,000 hectares of land make up England's Green Belt. This is 12 per cent of the area of England. (page 21)

⇨ A University of Glasgow study of nine areas around the country found that where local authorities make greenfield sites available, developers choose that land over brownfield sites. (page 22)

⇨ If you are under the age of 18, you will not be able to apply for a mortgage to buy accommodation. This is because you cannot own property in your own right, although it may be held in trust for you until you come of age. (page 26)

⇨ More than 300,000 new homes could be built, providing a £72.5 billion boost to the economy over ten years, through root and branch reform of the housing finance system, a report has revealed. (page 29)

⇨ Households buying a property through shared ownership earn an average of around £27,000 a year. (page 31)

⇨ A survey of over 1,800 people revealed that double the amount of 18 to 30 year olds – approximately a third (30.8%) – have rented three or four properties, whilst only 17.5% of Generation X had rented a similar number at the same age. (page 33)

⇨ In the early 1980s, council tenants' average income was 73 per cent of the national average. Today, two-thirds of social housing tenants are among the poorest 40 per cent of the population. (page 35)

⇨ At least 30% of housing in the proposed eco-towns will be affordable. (page 37)

GLOSSARY

Brownfield
A piece of land which has previously been developed, often abandoned or unused industrial sites. They can be redeveloped, but potential environmental contaminations mean this could be risky and expensive.

Community Self Build
This is where a group of men and women in housing need join forces and become involved in the planning, design and building of their own homes.

Eco-town
Eco-towns are proposed new communities to provide between 5,000 and 15,000 new homes. The Government says that the new developments will be affordable, well-designed, well-built and 'green' as well as linking to existing towns and having facilities such as schools, health centres, parks and allotments. However, critics say the new towns could devastate the countryside, may not be as green as the government suggests and could cause problems for commuters.

Green Belt
A designation for land surrounding certain large cities and built-up areas, designated as such with the aim of keeping the space open or mostly undeveloped.

Greenfield
This term refers to land which has not previously been built upon. It is often in the countryside.

Household
A group of people living together as a domestic unit.

Landlord
A home-owner who rents out (lets) their house to tenants.

Lodger
Someone renting a room in a household where they live alongside the home-owner(s).

Mortgage
A type of bank loan for buying a property. It is given against the value of the property, so inability to pay could result in eviction. There are a number of different types of mortgages available to those looking to buy a home, with different payment terms and rates of interest.

Nimbyism
Nimby is an acronym for 'Not In My Back Yard'. It is often used negatively to describe the attitudes of residents who oppose new developments close to them. While they may not object in principle to a development which will have benefits for many, they would wish it to be built elsewhere so it will not negatively affect or inconvenience them.

Repossession
If someone is not able to keep up their mortgage repayments, they can be evicted from their home, the ownership of which then reverts to the mortgage lender. This is called repossession.

Right to buy
A scheme which allows residents of council housing the right to buy the property they are living in. Critics say that the scheme has led to a shortage of social housing available to rent.

Self-help housing
Self-help housing involves people negotiating with the owners of empty properties to bring them back into use on a short term basis, until they're needed. This could be for a period of months or even years.

Shared ownership
Shared ownership offers eligible people the chance to buy between 25% and 75% of a property from a housing association, and pay an affordable rent on the remaining share. People can increase the share they own over time and ultimately own the property outright.

Social housing
Also called council housing, these are homes provided by the local authority or a housing association for rent. This is much cheaper than private renting and priority is given to applicants in housing need.

Squatting
Occupying an abandoned or empty building without the permission of the owner.

Stamp duty
A tax charged on properties valued at a certain amount (currently, this is under £175,001).

Sustainable housing
Buildings which have been designed with efficiency and environmental impact in mind are termed 'sustainable'.

Tenant
Someone living in rented accommodation.

Zero-carbon towns
The new eco-towns will be required to be zero-carbon over the course of a year, which means that during that period the net carbon emissions from all energy use by buildings in the development are zero.

INDEX

Additional Resources

Other Issues *titles*
If you are interested in researching further some of the issues raised in *The Housing Issue*, you may like to read the following titles in the **Issues** series:

⇨ Vol. 180 *Money and Finances* (ISBN 978 1 86168 504 9)

⇨ Vol. 160 *Poverty and Exclusion* (ISBN 978 1 86168 453 0)

⇨ Vol. 150 *Migration and Population* (ISBN 978 1 86168 423 3)

⇨ Vol. 149 *A Classless Society?* (ISBN 978 1 86168 422 6)

⇨ Vol. 146 *Sustainability and Environment* (ISBN 978 1 86168 419 6)

⇨ Vol. 130 *Homelessness* (ISBN 978 1 86168 376 2)

⇨ Vol. 97 *Energy Matters* (ISBN 978 1 86168 305 2)

For more information about these titles, visit our website at www.independence.co.uk/publicationslist

Useful organisations
You may find the websites of the following organisations useful for further research:

⇨ **ARLA:** www.arla.co.uk

⇨ **British Property Federation:** www.bpf.org.uk

⇨ **Citizens Advice:** www.adviceguide.org.uk

⇨ **Council of Mortgage Lenders:** www.cml.org.uk

⇨ **Home Builders Federation:** www.hbf.co.uk

⇨ **Inside Housing:** www.insidehousing.co.uk

⇨ **Local Government Association:** www.lga.gov.uk

⇨ **National Housing Federation:** www.housing.org.uk

⇨ **Policy Exchange:** www.policyexchange.org.uk

⇨ **PropertyLive:** www.propertylive.co.uk

⇨ **self-help-housing.org:** www.self-help-housing.org

⇨ **Shelter:** www.shelter.org.uk

⇨ **Straight Statistics:** www.straightstatistics.org

⇨ **TheSite:** www.thesite.org

ACKNOWLEDGEMENTS

The publisher is grateful for permission to reproduce the following material.

While every care has been taken to trace and acknowledge copyright, the publisher tenders its apology for any accidental infringement or where copyright has proved untraceable. The publisher would be pleased to come to a suitable arrangement in any such case with the rightful owner.

Chapter One: Housing Problems

First-time buyers wait to get on property ladder, © Telegraph Media Group Limited (2009), *Household projections to 2031, England,* © Crown copyright is reproduced with the permission of Her Majesty's Stationery Office, *Home building,* © Home Builders Federation, *Rural residents face 280-year wait for a home,* © Inside Housing, *Nearly a third of young men live with their parents,* © Crown copyright is reproduced with the permission of Her Majesty's Stationery Office, *Brits have given up hope of ever owning a home,* © PropertyLive.co.uk, *Affordable housing target will be missed,* © Guardian News & Media Ltd 2009, *Profiting from repossession,* © Guardian News & Media Ltd 2009, *Social housing waiting lists 'growing',* © National Housing Federation, *Growing up in social housing in Britain,* © Tenant Services Authority, *Who's living in my social housing?,* © Straight Statistics, *A third of households with children live in poor housing,* © Crown copyright is reproduced with the permission of Her Majesty's Stationery Office, *One million children overcrowded,* © Shelter, *Attitudes to social housing,* © Inside Housing, *New homes 'too small for everyday life',* © CABE (Commission for Architecture and the Built Environment), *Your rights as a tenant,* © TheSite, *Research reveals Britain's 'reluctant landlords',* © Association of Residential Letting Agents (ARLA), *Student accommodation,* © Lisa Firth/Independence, *Government clamps down on shared accommodation,* © British Property Federation, *Squatting,* © TheSite, *Green Belt,* © politics.co.uk, *Greenfield development trends,* © Telegraph Media Group Limited (2009).

Chapter Two: Housing Solutions

What political parties say about housing policy, © Times Newspapers Ltd, *Planning for buying a home,* © Crown copyright is reproduced with the permission of Her Majesty's Stationery Office, *Low-cost home-ownership options,* © Council of Mortgage Lenders, *Young people and housing,* © Citizens Advice, *Taking out a mortgage,* © Citizens Advice, *Reform housing system to build 300,000 new homes,* © Local Government Association, *Community Self Build,* © Community Self Build Agency, *Shared ownership,* © National Housing Federation, *Self-help housing – making use of empty properties,* © self-help-housing.org, *Gen Y wants freedom from flat ownership,* © Association of Residential Letting Agents (ARLA), *Housing poverty,* © Centre for Social Justice, *Give council tenants the right to move,* © Policy Exchange, *Eco-towns glossary,* © Crown copyright is reproduced with the permission of Her Majesty's Stationery Office, *An introduction to eco-towns,* © Crown copyright is reproduced with the permission of Her Majesty's Stationery Office, *Eco-towns approved amid country devastation fears,* © Telegraph Media Group Limited (2009), *Getting real about sustainable housing,* © Forum for the Future.

Photographs

Stock Xchng: pages 4 (Neil Hoskins); 5, 24, 35 (Ivan Petrov); 20 (Alexander Sperl); 30 (vailiki); 36 (Tory Byrne); 38 (Bev Lloyd-Roberts).
Wikimedia Commons: page 9 (Towerblocktom).

Illustrations

Pages 3, 12, 16: Don Hatcher; pages 6, 15, 27: Simon Kneebone; pages 8, 17: Bev Aisbett; pages 13, 21, 34: Angelo Madrid.

And with thanks to the team: Mary Chapman, Sandra Dennis, Claire Owen and Jan Sunderland.

Lisa Firth
Cambridge
September, 2009